FRAGMENTS OF PARADOX

FURTHER ZEN RAMBLINGS FROM THE INTERNET

SCOTT SHAW

BUDDHA ROSE PUBLICATIONS

Fragments of Paradox
Further Zen Ramblings from the Internet
Copyright © 2019 by Scott Shaw
www.scottshaw.com
ALL RIGHTS RESERVED

Cover Photographs by Scott Shaw
Copyright © 2019 All Rights Reserved

Rear Cover Photograph of Scott Shaw
by Hae Won Shin
Copyright © 2019 All Rights Reserved

First Edition 2019

This book contains material protected under International and Federal Copyright Laws and Treaties. Any unauthorized reprint or use of this material is prohibited. No part of this book may be reproduced or transmitted in any form or by any means, electronic or mechanical, including photocopying, recording, or by any information storage and retrieval system without express written permission from the author or publisher.

ISBN 10: 1-949251-14-4
ISBN 13: 978-1-949251-14-2

Library of Congress: 2019937958

10 9 8 7 6 5 4 3 2 1
Printed in the United States of America

FRAGMENTS OF PARADOX

Foreword

Throughout history there has been those who have sought to gain a deeper understanding of the mysteries of this universe.

Throughout time there has been those who have desired to refine their consciousness to the point where they may find an answer to the ultimate questions of humanity.

Throughout the course of human evolution there has been those who have chosen to leave behind the comforts of material existence and enter a path not dominated by the desires for material wealth and physical acquisitions. That path is known as *the Spiritual Path*.

The Spiritual Path, even the name promises the allure of mystery and profound understandings.

The Spiritual Path is not the path of one religion. Nor is *the Spiritual Path* owned by any one philosophy. *The Spiritual Path* is not defined by what a person wears or where they live. *The Spiritual Path* is place of consciousness. It is a metaphysical state of mind, where those who walk upon it are doing so to become a beacon of light in a sea of darkness.

The Spiritual Path is not a place. *The Spiritual Path* is a state of mind.

The Spiritual Path is not a road that can be transversed by everyone. Though there is no one requirement to enter *the Spiritual Path,* each of those who enter the path posses a unique calling that is not embraced by the masses.

Though many enter *the Spiritual Path,* most fall away.

There are as many reasons for veering away from *the Spiritual Path* as there are for beginning to walk upon it.

The pages of this book will hopefully provide those who choose to enter this road to mystery with a few thoughts that many allow them to remained focus on their path to rising human consciousness.

Introduction

Here it is, *The Scott Shaw Zen Blog 13.0, PART II* originally presented on the *World Wide Web*. All of the writings presented in this book were written between November of 2018 and March of 2019.

As was the case with the previously published volumes based upon *The Scott Shaw Zen Blog;* entitled: *Scribbles on the Restroom Wall*, *The Chronicles: Zen Ramblings from the Internet*, *Words in the Wind*, *Zen Mind Life Thoughts*, *The Zen of Life, Lies, and Aberrant Reality*, *Apostrophe Zen*, and *The Abstract Arsenal of Zen and the Psychology of Being*, *Zen and Again: The Metaphysical Philosophy of Psychology*, *Tempest in a Teapot and the Den of Zen*, *Buddha in the Looking Glass*, *Wo Ton' of the Blue Vision*, *Zen and the Psychology of the Spiritual Something*, and *Pyrophoric Zen* this volume is presented exactly as it was viewed on scottshaw.com with no rewriting, punctuation, or typo corrections. From this, we hope you will receive the original reading experience.

This volume of internet ramblings is presented with the date and time listed as to when each blog was originally posted. Also, the blogs in this volume are presented from last to first. With this, we hope to present a transcendence back through time as opposed to an evolving evolution. In addition, we left out the traditional *Table of Contents* in an attempt to leave this volume with a much more free-flowing reading experience.

Okay, there's the information and the definitions. Read on… We hope you enjoy it. And, be sure to stayed tuned for the ongoing *Scott Shaw Zen Blog* @ scottshaw.com.

Most People Are Not Trained That They Are Not Suppose To Embrace Their Ego
26/Mar/2019 08:45 AM

Most people are not trained to understand the fact that they are not supposed to embrace their ego. In fact, it is just the opposite. They are trained to take pride in how they look, what they accomplish, whom they overcome, and what they have.

There is a fatal flaw in this mindset, however. That flaw is that if you live your life from a position of ego-based existence, then you are always in a state of competition—you are forever battling to be the more and get the more. Plus, you are forced into a mind frame of being self-critical and constantly comparing yourself to others.

As has long been taught via the various spiritual traditions, one should remove themselves from the world ego existence. If one hopes to embrace Divine Consciousness then one should remove the concept of selfishness as the key component to a person's life. But, the fact is, most people don't care about exploring a deeper understanding of Self. They don't care about Comic Consciousness. All they want is what they want and to look the way they want to look and be who they want to be. Thus, they are damned to constantly be in a state of attempting to acquire and a state of dissatisfaction with what they currently have and who they actually are.

It has been spoken about for eons what a person should do and how they should behave if they hope to live a better, more enlightened life. But, who listens to those teachings? Who puts them into practice? Very few. Most people are simply content to live a life defined by conflict: internal and external—a life defined by winning and losing, having and wanting.

Think about this... Take a look at yourself. Take a look at how you have lived your life up until this point. Take a look at how you have interacted with and impacted the other people in your life. What is the essence of who you are? How have you gotten to where you are? What impact has how you have lived your life had on your life? And, what impact has how you have lived your life had on the lives of other people?

To answer... Many/most people step back from their responsibility in the process of defining who they are, what they have done, and whom they have done what to. They simply conclude, that's just who and what I am. That is what has been expected of me and/or this is what I have done with what I had. But, all that is simply excuses. Words used to keep yourself from not being mindful enough to take responsible for who and what you are and who and what you have done what to. This entire situation is commonly compounded when a person becomes successful in their craft. For then, they are operation from a space of pure ego. *"I am! Therefore I have power! Let me use my power to overpower you!"* Do you see the problem in all of this?

Most people do not care about anything but the ego-driven life-direction they have defined for themselves based upon the getting of what they want. As long as they look in the mirror and like what they see, as long as they are living the way they want to live, as long as they are moving in the direction they want, as long as they have people around them who desire them; love and support them, then all is good with their world. But, that is all ego. That is all based upon the illusion of the temporariness of the fulfilled desire.

People may thrive in one moment. But, that never lasts. People get knocked down, that is just the reality of life. People get old. People spend their money. Loved ones and family members die. Times change and what was liked and loved at one point in history is shunned at another. Then what? What happens next? Who are you when you don't like what you see in the mirror, you have lost what you achieved, or others no longer care about you? People deny this will ever happen, but it always happens. One way or the other when you base your life on the selfish pursue of ego-driven reality, then loss is the one promised outcome.

Most people never take the time to look at their ego and witness how they are an ego-driven being. Do you? Do you ever take the time to study how you think about yourself, how you see yourself during interaction(s) with your society and other people, how and why you project yourself in a particular fashion to the external world?

You are the creator of you. You can create from a space of refined consciousness or you can create based simply upon your ego-driven desires. But, knowing that the you that is currently you will never last—knowing that the you who is you is only the illusion that you project to the world, who is it that you will ultimately become by following the path that you are walking along? Is your road defined by your ego or is it defined by embracing the Greater More?

It is only you who has the power to put your ego in check. Will you allow yourself to take control or will your allow your ego to guide you through you life?

Jesus and Accolades After You're Dead
25/Mar/2019 08:11 AM

There is certainly no other figure of modern history that has been discussed and worshiped more than Jesus Christ. For the past two thousand years no one else has been for the focus of more prayer, more war, or more belief than Jesus Christ. But, virtually all that happened because of and due to Jesus Christ happened after his assentation—after he left his physical body.

Except for the Bible, there is little else that anyone can turn to for a discussion of the life of Jesus Christ. Forget about the historic debate of Jesus, we will simply take the accepted historic understanding of Jesus Christ at face value.

Did Jesus live a good life? Well, no one really knows much about the life he lived up until the later stage of his physical existence. But, from that point forward was his life good? From a purely physical perspective, probably not. There was a lot of conflict and controversy surrounding him. Ending in his being put to death on the cross. A symbol that is today worn around the neck of millions of his followers.

From a Christian perspective, it is believed that Jesus is looking down on; guiding and protecting all of the believers. Millions pray to him for guidance on a daily basis. Even more worship him. But, when he was alive how many people were his followers? How many people believed in his teachings? How many people prayed to him? Very few, if any. Yet, today, he is the most worshiped deity on the planet. But, during his life, he personally, in his physical form, did not encounter any of that. He never knew, on a physical level, what it was like to be loved and revered by the people of his time period.

When someone is dead can they truly experience the love or admiration that other people have for them?

Have you notice that when someone passes away; maybe someone who did something nice for humanity, was a teacher, was very creative, or was well liked, all of sudden people get together and commentate them, maybe give them a posthumous award, or something like that? That's all nice and everything... But, the problem is, that person is dead. They can't really experience the love coming their direction or the giving of the givers. So, what does it all mean? Who is receiving the gift if the person the gift is intended for is not alive to accept it and appreciate it?

We all believe in who and what we believe in. We all like and respect whom we like and respect. Some, perhaps even many of those people are no longer alive. So, what does our love and admiration for that person actually equal?

It is important that we begin to chart a better course for those people who are alive; those people who have helped us; those people we respect; those people who have influenced us; those people we like and/or love. We need to express our admiration while they are alive. We need to let them know that they are appreciated. We need to go out of our way, reach out a hand, and tell them, *"Thank you,"* by whatever method you choose to express that feeling.

When a person is dead, they are dead. Though they may be remembered, it is only when they are alive that they can truly interactively experience the fact that what they have done was like, appreciated, or helped to help someone in someway.

While they are alive, reach out to the people who have given your life something. Do what you can to make them know that you appreciate their existence. Do this before it is too late.

*   *   *
25/Mar/2019 08:09 AM

Do you believe what someone says simple because they say it?

If you do then you have lost the beauty of self exploration.

* * *

24/Mar/2019 07:55 AM

It only takes one person to instigate an entire deluge of negativity.

It only takes one person to instigate an entire deluge of positivity.

The Case of Consideration
23/Mar/2019 04:15 PM

My lady and I were sitting outside at a Starbucks, enjoying an afternoon latte, when this SUV pulls up right in front of where we are sitting. A person gets out and goes inside. The couple inside the car continues to sit there, laughing and joking, parked in the red, as the other passing cars must cautiously navigate their way around the vehicle. First my lady notices it and then I do; this car's exhaust is directly pouring onto us, destroy the air we breathe.

I started to become annoyed and wonder if I should go and say something. Just then, the person who went inside walks outside and starts to do these weird stretching exercises not far from our table. He then walks over to the window of the SUV, which the passenger rolls down, and laughingly tells them he is still waiting for their drinks. The window is rolled back up so they can embrace the air-conditioned comfort as we sit there bombarded by their exhaust.

Finally, I say, *"Fuck it, let's go."* There we were, the driver and the passenger(s) ruined our afternoon experience. Did they even think about us or consider the cars they were causing to cautiously drive around them? Nope. They just parked in the red, not thinking or caring about anyone but themselves; wanting to be as close to the front door of Starbucks as possible.

Now, I could have gone up and gotten in their business. But, I long ago learned that when you tell someone they are doing something wrong, generally all they do is either deny it, not care, or come back at you as if you were the one who is doing something wrong, causing the entire situation to escalate. I just didn't need it…

So, here's the question? How often do you do something that hurts the moment or the entire life of someone else? How often do you take the other person into consideration? How often do you think about how your actions are going to affect someone else? How often do you deny wrongdoing when you are the one doing something wrong? How often do you care about anyone but yourself, whether you know them or not?

Every moment of everyone's life is affected by the someone else who does the something else. Do you ever think about this before you do what you do?

* * *
23/Mar/2019 09:21 AM

We all have a story to tell.

I Hate To Say I Told You So. But...
23/Mar/2019 08:42 AM

The space and time we live in has brought us a new and unique set of challenges for walking the path of self-betterment, consciousness, and self-realization. In many ways, everything has become so much easier. Whether this is researching life and life-ideologies, reading books, finding our entertainment, or even making a living; it is all right in front of us on our phones or on our computers. There is a problem that has arisen with this new technology, as well, however. That problem is, self-empowerment. As everybody now has the ability to easily gain knowledge, make money, and find people of like mind, they also have the eased ability of creating (for lack of a better term) bad karma. Why? Because there is no filter. People can say and/or do whatever they want with little or no consequences.

Many people have come to thrive in this new technology driven environment. And, that's not a bad thing. But, what many a person does not see or even contemplate is what will happened to them farther, in some cases much farther, down the road of their life if they have built their existence, their friendships, and even their livelihood upon hurting anyone—even one person.

People live their life in the moment. This is why I have long stated that the entire New Age concept of, *"Being in the Now,"* is false. As everybody is already always in the Now. Everyone is always thinking about the Now: how they are feeling Now, what they are doing Now, and how this Now can provide them with what they want in their next Now.

Okay... So, we all are already living in the Now. The problem(s) arise, however, in what you do in this Now. What you say in this Now, what you organize in this Now, what you prepare in this Now, what you live in this Now, who you live with in this Now, who you interact with in this Now, and how your Now affects your life and the life of other people.

Certainly, there are those people who are truly caring, giving individuals out there. They are the ones who should be saluted. Sure, their caring and their giving also provides themselves with a positive brain response, but what they are doing sets a course of help and positivity into motion. But, how many people are like that? How many people go out of their way to help? How many people go out of their way to countermand, in a positive way, the negativity unleashed by others? Most people are simply doing what they are doing to make themselves feel a specific way in their Now. They are doing what they are doing to make money in their Now. They are doing what they are doing for themselves and for the people they like and care about in their Now. As long as they are fulfilled; as long as their Now and their Promised Tomorrow are in a seemingly good place, who cares about anyone else or the people they step on to keep their okay feeling okay in their Now.

There is a problem in all of this *Self-Nowness,* however. That problem is, as long a person is only thinking about themselves, they are only thinking about themselves—they are not taking other people into consideration. And, here/this is where all of the problems of life begin.

Look to the news on any day of the week and you will see some person: be they rich, a star, or a criminal who at one point had the world by the tail but now they have fallen from grace. How and why did this happen? There are a million reasons, but the one thing that is clear is that, in their assention they either hurt or did not care about other people.

In my own life, I have watched as many a person who was once at the top fall painfully to the bottom of the heap. In each case, the reason for this was different, but the one common thread was that the specific person only cared about himself or herself and damaged the life of other people in their assent to the top.

In my own life, I have also watched as a very few people, who lived a good and caring life, passed positively through their life. It was those people who never experienced that painful fall from grace.

As I say over and over again, everything in life begins with you. It begins with what you do.

We all want to live a good life. But, how we choose to get to live that good life will set our final destiny into motion.

Good or bad begins with the small things that you do. Saying good and positive things equals good and positive things. Saying negative, hurtful, or judgmental things equals pain and negativity.

How much pain have you caused someone else as you have passed through your life doing what you wanted to do; getting what you wanted to get, and reaching where you wanted to be? You want to predict where you are going to end up in your life—you want to know what will befall you? Look to every bad, negative, hurtful, or judgmental word you have spoken, look to every hurtful deed you have done, look to everything you have taken that was not yours, look to everyone you have hurt.

Stop lying to yourself that your Now is the only Now that matters. If your Now has or is hurting someone else's Now, how do you think that will ultimately affect your life?

Where will you be when your Now is not the way you wanted your Now to be? Remember to ask yourself when you get to a place where your Now is not the way you wanted your Now to be, *"What did I do to cause me to arrive at this point in my life?"*

Think. Think about yourself. Think about what you are doing and why. Think about others.

*   *   *

22/Mar/2019 12:59 PM

How many people should you be allowed to hurt in life?

*   *   *

22/Mar/2019 07:09 AM

Do you ever take the other person into consideration?

* * *

20/Mar/2019 03:47 PM

If you steal, you've stolen.

If you give, you've given.

Which do you think is better?

*   *   *
20/Mar/2019 09:06 AM

How much of what you do in your life equals nothing?

Life Remembered
19/Mar/2019 09:43 AM

There is this small field out in front of where I live. Periodically, a group of feral cats comes to live there. Where they come from—their origin, I never know. Every now and then they just show up. I guess someone just dumps them there. Sad, I think. Animals are so great. They deserve better. They deserved to be loved and cared for.

Anyway, there was this group of kittens that came to inhabit the field a while back. There were five. It was really fun to watch them from above. They would run and play and explore—living life from the mindset of the new and the uncharted.

They were black and white in color. I could tell which one was which one by their individual markings. I watched them grow.

Then, as always, whenever a new crew of kittens arrives, I wish that there was more that I could for them. But, you can't really capture and incarcerate a feral cat, as for them, that would just be a prison. My one neighbor does put out food and water for them. That's a good thing, I think. I'm sure that helps them out.

Sometimes, I would see two or more of them curled up and sleeping together out in the field. Keeping each other warm and reminding each other that they were not alone. Love and family is great !!!

This has been a very cold and wet winter here in So. Cal. Certainly, there are many places across the States that are much colder and wetter, but it has been noticeable very cold this year. I've heard it has been the coldest winter in over one-hundred years. I often thought about the cats living out there in the cold and the rain, wondering how and where do they take shelter.

As the winter has gone on, the number of cats has diminished. Now, there is only one left. One, all alone. I don't know what happened to his littermates. I can only imagine that they are gone due to this cold, wet winter. But he (or she) is now all alone. That must be really hard. I see him (or her) sitting out in the spot where they would cuddle up in times gone past. Now, this beautiful cat is all alone.

I can't claim that I know how cats think. But, having owned cats for many years I do know that they have very strong emotions and a long-term memory. So, I believe, it must be really hard for that cat to be out there all alone. He (or she) must remember that it was not always that way. That once upon a time there was someone to cuddle up with, someone to love.

I don't know... Lost is sad. Losing your family is sad. Losing the one's you love is sad. Being all alone is sad. It's even sadder when there is nothing that you can do to bring back the someone that someone once loved and make everything better. Alone is never a good thing.

Right now, I look out my window and the cat is sitting in the field, the spot where they used to cuddle up. He (or she) is sitting there all alone, staring off into the distance. Very sad...

* * *

17/Mar/2019 07:35 PM

Would you lie if your lie hurt someone else?

Showing Your Hand
17/Mar/2019 12:44 PM

For the advanced poker player, they have an expression for the player who has a, *"Tell,"* when they have a good or a bad hand. They call it, *"Showing your hand."* The true poker player always looks for this in other players because it helps them chart their next play in the game.

Personally, I've never really been much of a poker player. I'm just not a gambler by nature. Sure, I know how to play—at least some of the more common styles of poker and have played (for fun, not money) a few times with my friends and family in younger days. But, I also know those people who are avid players. They are really in there to win. They look for the other player, *"Showing their hand."*

In life, it is very much like this, as well. There are the people who know how to disguise what they think and what they do. They know how to protect themselves and their thoughts. But, then there are those who, whether knowingly or not, broadcast to the world who they truly are on the inside. They do this, and for anyone with an eye for detail, their, *"Tell,"* can be seen.

In the world of creativity, I have observed this many a time. There is the person who claims all of this ability and/or all of this knowledge but when you look at their output, all they have done is, at best, mimic what someone else has already done. Or, in some cases, the just flat out steal the words, the ideas, and/or the philosophy of someone else. They do this because they have no ability to formulate their own creative and philosophic ideology and, thus, they must steal someone else's.

Then, more often than not, they go after the person they have stolen from and find ways to criticize or diminish that person, their artistic vision, and their creativity. This, because they hope to control the mind's of others and how they interpret the person they have stolen from.

How about you? Do you create? If you do create, do your rob the words, the thoughts, and the creative vision of someone else? Or, is what you create wholly organic and pure? Is it your own?

Moreover, when you seek guidance in understanding the creative process, whom do you turn to for information? Do you form your own opinions based upon your own beliefs and realizations or do you base what you think about a particular someone or something upon the words conveyed by someone else?

Your life is defined by what you create while you are alive. Your life is defined by the information you disseminate in life based upon what others have created and how it has influenced you. If you cannot be your own person, if you cannot be whole and true to the fact of what you have created and/or whom you have borrowed what form, then you are nothing more than a liar. A thief who is not whole and honest enough to footnote your influences. This is one of the ultimate sins in the game of life. And, for those who are aware enough to study what you do and what you have done it will become the definition of how others interpret your existence. Though you may be able to steal a word here or a thought there, if you cannot site your references, if you cannot give credit where credit is due, then who are you? What are you? Are you yourself or are you simply a mirror of that other person?

Is a mirrored image real or is it simply an illusion?

* * *

17/Mar/2019 07:12 AM

How often do you think about another person before you do what you do?

How often do you think about what your actions will mean to another person before you do what you do?

How often to you think about the people you know?

How often do you think about the people you don't know?

Life is defined by what you think and who you think about.

The actions you take are defined by what you think and who you think about.

Where you end up in life is defined by what you think and who you think about.

What people think about you is defined by what you think and who you think about.

Isn't it time to start thinking about someone else other than you yourself?

The Doing of Bad Things
16/Mar/2019 09:26 AM

For most of us, we pass through our life doing the best that we can while hopefully having a bit of fun, happiness, and companionship. We care about the people we care about, we do our jobs, whether we love them or hate them, and we put our time in at life while leaving little in our wake. Some people step to the pulpit. They are heard more than others. They say what they say based upon what they believe. Some even rise to the top of their individualizes professions. How do they get there? Well, that is a query that will be forever debated. But, none-the-less, they do. Most, however, are not that fortunate, they simply exist, dominated by the trends of life, society, and the forces that control all of us.

Though no one is perfect. There is no one who does good, righteous, and perfect things all of the time, most of us never set out to hurt anyone. This is especially the case, as we get older in life. As we age we come to see the implications of our actions. We come to understand how doing bad things to one person not only hurts the life of that person but, in the end, it also damages our own life, as well. Thus, through trial, error, and enhanced experiential understanding, we try to become the best person that we can be; doing good things and not bad things.

In this modern age, we are bombarded with information coming at us from all angles. We are quite frequently reminded that there is a subgroup of people out there doing some pretty bad things. These bad things span the gambit of the definition of bad, and we heard about them all of the time.

Currently, it is often spoken about that there is a new breed of terrorist, a new level of people finding a way to find their way to fame via doing bad things. Though we are embraced by new and enhanced informational technology all of the time, the doing of bad things is not new to human culture. Yes, there are new ways to broadcast and/or take credit for the doing of bad things. Yes, there are new ways to get famous for doing bad things. Yes, there are new ways to disseminate the information about how to do bad things. But, the doing of bad things has gone on forever. Some people got away with it, some people didn't. But, at the end of each person's life, all you will be defined by is what you have done. Some people believe in the judgment of god or karma, some people don't. But, whatever the state of one's belief system is, if a person cannot be self-evolved enough to understand that it is bad to say and/or do bad things that hurts someone, anyone else, then what does that say about them as a human being?

As we look to the lives of the people that hurt others, we can see that each of these people have a self-defined understand that allows them to believe that what they are doing is right. Some have even claimed that they are doing the bad things that they are doing to help a culture, a race, or a religion. Others just do bad things because it makes them feel good. But, whatever the motivation, if a person targets one of more people and devises a game plan to hurt that one or more people, they become defined by the very action that they are taking. They are doing something bad to someone and no matter what their motivation is, what they are doing is wrong by all definitions of true human understanding.

As we pass though life we will all encounter the badness that other people do. For some, this sadly may take on a personal understanding when something bad is done to you. But, whether it is on the personal level or on a global scale, each person's life is each person's life. Does that person want something bad to be done to them? Does the person who is doing something bad want something bad done to them? No. No one does. And, this should be the definition about how you encounter life and how you treat other people, either on the singular, personal level or on the global scale.

At each position of your life, in each situation that you encounter, you can make a decision to say or do something positive or you can make a decision to say or do something hurtful. You can applaud badness or you can countermand it. You are in control of yourself. Thus, you must make the conscious decision about what you can and will do.

As we pass through our life we are each going to encounter situation that we like or dislike, we are each going to encounter people that we like or dislike. But, if you allow your emotions towards a situation or a person to cause you to do something bad, all that does is to add to the ongoing damage that is prevalent in this world. Just because you like or dislike something or someone why does that give you the right to hurt that something or someone? If you do hurt that something or someone, how does that make you any different then person who unleashes a devastating massive attack on a culture, a race, or a religion?

Some people take pride in their ability to damage the life of another person or hurt some larger something that they do not like. But, what about the person who is hurt? Don't they have feelings too? What about the larger entity that is hurt? Doesn't it serve its own purpose?

Hurt only equals hurt. Badness only equals badness. The small things in life that people choose to do are what sets the stage for what other people do. You can be a beacon of goodness or you can applaud the badness. You can take part in the goodness and make everything a little bit better—one small thing at a time. Or, you can embrace the badness. Remember to question, at the end of your everything what will your badness have equaled? Only hurt. Only badness. A person who does something bad to even one person will always be defined by the hurt that they unleashed. Do you think that is a good thing? Choose goodness.

Wanting What You Don't Have
15/Mar/2019 08:05 AM

More often then not, I get a lot a of requests from a lot of people asking me to give them copies of my movies, my books, and my music. In more recent times, I have been receiving a lot of requests for video tape copies of my movies as the resurgence of VHS tapes, among underground communities, has become the latest rage. Asking is fine. Giving is fine. I am happy to give people something if I have something to give. But, the fact of the matter is, rarely do I have copies of what people are asking for.

In some cases, it is kind of amusing to chart the reaction of people when I tell them I don't have a copy. Some people don't believe me and keep coming back asking again and again. Some people are sure that I'm wrong and ask me to check again. Some people even think that I'm lying to them and that I simply don't want to give them a copy.

I certainly have given a lot of copies of a lot of stuff away. If I have it and someone asks, I give. But, I already have given all of my copies away.

One of the funny thing is, people assume that it is all free for me. ...That I created the something so the VHS, the DVD, the CD, the book, or even the Headshot that they want me to sign, is free. But, the fact of life is, just because you create something does not mean that it is free. No matter who you are, you have to pay somebody something for anything. So, the movies, the music, the anything, once it is on something, it costs money to make. Who should pay for what?

But, that's all okay. I get it. People want. That's the human condition. Whatever the reason for somebody wanting something is a personal thing but you can't give them what you don't have.

A funny side note here is, a few years back this one guy contacted me and asked me to send him a free copy of one of my *Zen Films* as he wanted to review it. The thing was, this guy had already written a very critical, completely factually inaccurate, article about me and posted it on a website—a real hatchet job. He really went after me based upon false assumptions and lies. In his ask for the movie he stated that he had only watched the movie from an unauthorized download site and he didn't think it would be fair to review the movie unless he owned a copy. There he was, a guy who had previously gone out of his way to write a horrible article about me, accusing me of being morally wrong and a generally terrible person, but what he had already done was far more reprehensible. Internet Piracy is not a Victimless Crime! As amusing as I found this entire situation, I obviously did not send him a copy. I don't even think I had a copy.

This all goes to the point and the parcel of life. People want. People want what they want. And, many/most of them want it free.

Sure, everybody has their own reason for wanting what they want. Sure, everyone has a reason for wanting it for free. But, you can't give what you don't have. And, this goes to so many levels of existence.

Think about your own life. Think about the things that people have wanted from you that you could not give. Think about the things that you wanted from others that they could not give you. Did it stop them from wanting? Did it stop you from wanting? What did they do when they couldn't get what they wanted from you? What did you do when you couldn't get what you wanted from them?

People do all kind of things based upon what they want. Some of them are not good. Some of them cause crisis in the life of the wanter and the life of the wanted. But, wanting is what people want. So, all you can do is give when you can. But, you can't give what you don't have!

I know that it has been one of my liabilities in life, as well. …That I go out of my way to make, create, duplicate, and do things to give people what they want. But, what does the fulfillment of anyone else's desire equal if it hurts your own life? Think about that when you want something from someone. Think about that when someone wants something from you. You can't give what you don't have.

A Buddhist is an Atheist
14/Mar/2019 08:36 AM

Certainly, no one can deny that religion is one of the driving forces of this planet earth. Though many people have moved away from formal religion that is not the case for most. People want to believe! People want to believe that there is a purpose for their life. People want to believe that by behaving in a good way they will be rewarded in the afterlife. People want to believe that they can turn to a supreme being and receive guidance and help. That's fine. Each person should believe as they wish to believe.

In each culture, a specific religion is programmed into a young child. What the parents believe is what the child is taught to believe. This is what has kept religious traditions alive.

In a few cases, there has been a vast shift in a religion at a specific point in history. This was certainly the case with Christianity growing out of Judaism and Buddhism rising out of Hinduism. In Christianity there arose one figure that came to define the religion, Jesus. This is the same with Buddhism. The ironic thing is, however, this was not the Buddha's teachings. He taught of a mental landscape void of idol worship. Yet, look at his legacy, there are statues of the Buddha everywhere, people pray to the Buddha everywhere, and people look to the Buddha for guidance. Though these people consider themselves Buddhists, they have missed the entire point of what the Buddha taught. They do not practice the techniques of removing their mind from the constraints of the material world and thereby encountering nirvana, they simply pass through their life worshiping an idealize image of a person they believe possess the ultimate understanding.

So, what does this tell us about religion, religious teachers, and the human society as a whole? It teaches us that most people do not and/or cannot remove themselves from the constraints of everyday life. They do not want to. They are content being dominated by the external while avoiding the internal. They do not possess the mental wherewithal to transcend from common existence and move into a space of ultimate understanding. This is not right or wrong; it is simply the definition of human society.

This then leads us to one of the ultimate questions of life. For you, as a living person, what do you believe? Do you ever take the time to question this question? Do you ever take the time to study where your belief system arose? Where did you learn what you believe? And, why do you believe what you were taught to believe? Moreover, is what you believe the actual teachings of the instigator and source point of what you believe? Are you believing/are you practicing what the founder of your religion actually taught? Because if you are not, then you are not a true practitioner of the religion at all. Where does that leave you?

Rewarding Bad Behavior
13/Mar/2019 09:01 AM

In society, particularly at this point in history where we find ourselves, we are constantly being told about the bad behavior of some person—particularly a celebrity. There are news articles, documentaries, and commentaries put out there all of the time. Though these are sometimes interesting, it is essential to note that they are commonly very one sided interpretations of what has taken place in a person's life—they are, none-the-less, ideal examples of the bad behavior that takes place around us all of the time.

Though the celebrities are often times the only ones who are newsworthy, bad behavior goes on all the time all across the globe. Why are the celebrities discussed with such fervor? Because by talking about them there is money to be made. Speak about someone that no one knows and no one will listen. Speak about a celebrity and everyone will have an opinion. Simply by mentioning their name there will instantly be detractors and supporters. But, what are these emotions based upon? The person who feels them did not know the person. The person who feels them had no experiences: good or bad with the person. Yet, they are motived to feel. But, why?

If we look across this planet there are people doing bad things all of the time. There are people being hurt, there are people being damaged, there are people being stolen from, and there are people being killed. There is a bad person doing bad things probably every second of every day. How about you? Do you do bad things?

Now, here is where it gets interesting. Very bad things are done by people all of the time. In recent times many of these people have been called out for their bad behavior—bad behavior that a decade or two or three ago was simply considered, the way that it was... Plus, there are the very bad deeds that put people in prison. But, what about the everybody else? What about you? What about the bad things that you do?

Some people, in fact most people, never look at the bad things that they do. In fact, many do not even consider the implications of their actions. If they can get away with it, they are all good. For example, people steal things all the time on the internet. They file share music, they watch movies from off shore websites, they plagiarize, they copy and use other people photos and art, you name it... But, do the people that do this consider their actions bad behavior. No. Why should they? They are an anonymous person in a vast cyber world and everybody else is doing it, so... But, is the crime any the less?

At the root of all bad behavior is the person who believes that what they are doing is okay. Whether it is the celebrity treating women badly, sleeping with under age children, beating up a girlfriend, or stealing someone else's creation, they think what they are doing is okay. They can get away with it so it must be okay. How is that any different than the person who downloads a pirated song or a movie from the internet?

People always justify their crimes. Whether it is the person who is hungry stealing food from a store, the person who needs money to buy drugs so they rob somebody, the person who likes to fight so they look for someone weaker to beat up, the guy who likes sex with young women, the pedophile, or the person who steals the smallest item, bad is bad. Bad behavior is bad behavior and it leads to bad things. And, bad things lead to more bad things.

As I say over-and-over again, all life begins with you. All life begins with what you do. All life spreads outwards from you. There are bad things going on all over the world. There are bad people doing very bad things everyday. There are also people doing bad things that they, themselves, do not even take notice of. They do not even consider themselves doing a bad thing. How about you? Do you think about what you do? Do you consider the impact of what you do? Do you care about how what you do affects other people? If you don't, you are a bad person doing bad things.

The celebrities are often rewarded for bad behavior. They do something bad yet their fans come to their defense. But, does that make what they have done any less bad? In the movies and in music, it's always the, *"Bad guy,"* who comes off as the coolest. It is always the person who gets away with it that is idolized. But, did who they hurt in the doing of what they did even come into the storyline?

Every time something bad is done, someone is hurt. Every time you do something bad, someone is hurt. Is that right? Do you like it when someone hurts you?

You can reward bad behavior. You can practice bad behavior. But, bad is never good. Think about what you do, the implications of what you do, and how what you do will affect someone else. Think about the way you would feel if someone did that to you. And maybe, just maybe, you will not do that something bad and the world will become just a little bit better.

*   *   *

12/Mar/2019 01:44 PM

Religion is the ultimate way to get people to behave the way you want them to behave.

*   *   *

12/Mar/2019 11:03 AM

If you make somebody feel something you are responsible for what they are feeling.

* * *
12/Mar/2019 09:41 AM

When you find that you are unhappy do you ever question why you are unhappy?

The general answer will be that you are not getting what you what.

Is what you want selfish?

If it is then you should let go of your unhappiness.

Dislikes and Likes
12/Mar/2019 08:19 AM

Have you ever experienced the situation where you meet somebody for the first time and they immediately don't like you? As far as you can tell there is really no reason for this. You had never met them before, you never said anything to them, you never did anything to them, but they just do not like you. Why is that?

I suppose there are a million possible reasons for this condition. But, the primary factor is that they are feeling something and they are directing that something towards you. A something you, personally, had nothing to do with creating.

Whenever this has happened to me it has always surprised me. By nature, I am a smiley, happy-go-lucky, positive sort of guy. So, when I encounter negativity, directed my direction, it always sends me to wondering why.

As stated, there are a million possible reasons for a person feeling a certain way about another person that they do not know. I first began to see this in my youth when I was the only Caucasian kid in my neighborhood. More than a few times I encountered African-Americans hating me simply because I was White. But, even as a child I could understand the motivation for that. But still, they were basing their judgment of me on something I had nothing to do with creating. Then, as now, I was the happy, nice, caring person I have always been. But, in some cases, they didn't take the time to find that out.

As I became older and became part of the counter culture people would often hurl insults my direction because I had long hair, *"Faggot,"*

"Hippie," "Freak," and so on were the words they would commonly use. There were times when my friends and I would go into restaurants and we would not even be served and, in some cases, were asked to leave simply because we had long hair. And, this was in Los Angeles. Think what it was like in other parts of the country.

Again, people see an image and form a judgment based upon that image. They did not know or care who I was but they formed that judgment, based upon an external image.

As I moved forward into the world of creativity, I also periodically encountered people who disliked me for some unknown reason. But then, they would state that their judgment was based on the fact that they didn't like my art, my music, my movies, my writings, or my martial arts. Okay… But, that is not liking a something. Those somethings are something but they are not me. Why hate me for something I created?

There may be a million reasons for a person wishing to judge the creative works of another person and finding a reason to love or hate that person based upon that creation but without knowing the person who created them, and already forming an opinion about that person, something is truly lost in pure and truthful interactive consciousness.

Of course, there are always the people who are not mindful enough to form their own opinions about an individual. They hear what someone else has said and they believe that person at their word.

This is very dangerous, I believe. For simply believing what someone else has said removes personal understanding from the equation and relinquishes the decision making to the mind of someone else. ...The mind of someone else who you can never truly be sure why they are saying the what they are saying.

In my life, particularly in the world of the film industry and the martial arts, I have encountered this pre-judgment based mindset a number of times. Someone didn't like me because of what someone else has said. The question I always want to ask these people is, *"Why did that person say that?" "What was their motivation?"* And, *"Was what they were saying true?"* Commonly, when the facts are known, words were spoken simply to make the speaker look more and to make me look less or to ruin the chances of the other person and myself forming a friendship as that may invade on the current relationship. But, was what was spoken the truth or simply the projection from a less-evolved mind? If you listen to what other people say about another person you always must be careful to calculate why they are saying what.

More than someone simply not liking a person because of the color of their skin, their hair style, what they are wearing, or their creativity, at times some people just do not like someone just because... The because of <u>what</u> can forever be debated. But, they meet someone and immediately don't like them. This has always been the hardest for me to comprehend. Why do people form a judgment about a person they do not know?

There is the other side of the issue, of course. There are those who immediately love you for no apparent reason. In some way, this is more understandable, however. Maybe they like the way you look, appreciate your style, or are attracted to you. But, if a person likes you due to those factors this can always be seen by the way the other person presents himself or herself to you. You can see it in their eyes and feel it in their demeanor.

Of course, if you have created something—something that the other person likes or appreciates, this is the opposite of the person who doesn't like you for what you created. They like you for what you have created and they want to get to know you because of that fact. Maybe they wish to become part of your process or learn from you. Maybe they even want to make money from you.

Again, we can come back to the central point of this piece, people disliking or liking a person that they do not even know.

I imagine that we all do this to varying degrees, but for most of us we do it from a space of refined consciousness; we can describe that what we are feeling is based on a specific something. But, to the point, why like anyone? Why dislike anyone? What does that provide your life? And, why do you allow your likes or your dislikes to dominate what you do and how you feel?

The answer, many people are afraid to look inside. Many people are afraid to know themselves. Why take the time to know and refine yourself when it is so much easy to simply be control by whatever emotional emotion you are feeling. That is so much easier. That is so much more fun.

A truly consciousness person takes the time to chart their feelings, their emotions, and their judgments back to the source. From this, they most commonly realize that any judgment, be it positive or negative, that they hold towards another person is based in their own preconceived ideology. Yes, they may like what they like. Yes, they may dislike what they dislike. But, if you do not take the time to understand why you feel the way you feel, ultimately who you truly are is lost. And, all you become is a person guided by undefined emotions that not only have the potential to damage your own life but to damage the life of all of those that you judge without even knowing them.

The Things You Can't Undo
11/Mar/2019 08:57 AM

Have you ever done something and later regretted it? Have you ever behaved in a certain manner, at a specific point in time, and later wished that you had not behaved in the way that you behaved? Have you ever done something where you truly embarrassed yourself? Have you ever done something that later hurt your reputation when the truth about your actions came out? Have you ever hurt someone and later became a more evolved and less selfish human being which made you truly regret that you did what you did to that person? On varying levels, I believe that all of us have felt this way at one time or another in our lives.

But then, there is the other side of the coin. There are those people who do all kinds of damage to their own life and to the life of others and, for whatever reason, do not even care. Those people are few and far between, however. Most of us live an existence where we try, we evolve, we care, we think about ourselves, our lives, and other people; we think about how other people think about us. From this, our actions have consequences, even if those consequences are only in our own mind.

Right now, take a moment, and think about something that you did that you wish you could undo.

Right now, take a moment, and think about something that you did to someone else that you wish you could undo.

Right now, take a moment, and think about a situation where someone told you that you hurt them but you did nothing to repair the damage.

Which of those questions becomes the clearest in your mind? What you did that did something to yourself? Or, what you did that did something to someone else? The answer to this is going to tell you a lot about yourself.

Okay, you've done something that you see and feel is wrong. What did you do about it? What could you do about it then? What can you do about it now?

Many people simply hide from the fact of their misdeeds. Many people simply lie about, deny, or conceal their misdeeds. Many people surround themselves with a group of people that cheer on their misdeeds. But, wrong is always wrong. Whether you hurt yourself by what you have done or hurt others by your actions, what you did that was wrong never changes. It was wrong. You may see it as wrong. You may not. But, if you cannot chart your wrongness, if you cannot accept what you have done, all that happens is that you live a life based upon denial of the truth and that is never a good thing.

So, where does this leave us? What do we do about what we have done that is wrong? First of all, we have to acknowledge it. We must accept it. We have to view it for what it is. We have to analyze it and question ourselves why we did it in the first place. Then, we must be truthful to ourselves and to others.

The next step is action. Action is what caused you to do it in the first place. It is only through action, not denial, which will fix that what has been wronged.

Certainly, as we pass through life, we each do something that we wish we hadn't done. But, if we do not contemplate that action and what set us on that course to take that action, we can never correct our actions and thus we will continue to make the same mistake(s) over and over again.

A conscious person lives a conscious life. A caring person lives a caring life. Even a person who only cares about himself or herself, cares about how others care about them. Because it only from others that they gain the emotional and material support that they desire.

The root of all bad is in what you do and how you do it. The root of all wrong is in what you do and how you do it. If you cannot accept that you have done something wrong, if you cannot set about on course to fix the wrong you have done, your entire life becomes defined by that wrong no matter if it was done one minute ago or a hundred years ago.

Acknowledge that what you have done is wrong and/or has wronged others. Analyze why you did what you did. Fix it if you can. ...Care enough to fix it if you can. And, know yourself. Know why you do what you and why you did what you did. From this, hopefully, you will no longer instigate actions that you regret and you cannot undo.

* * *

11/Mar/2019 07:30 AM

Life is a Spiritual Path.

Whether or not you choose to travel through life consciously is almost unimportant, because life is a process of realization and awakening. Whether or not you choose to allow life-realization(s) to happen, they will occur.

Those who walk the Spiritual Path simply make this process a science and not merely random occurrences.

* * *
09/Mar/2019 02:28 PM

If your life is cluttered then your live is cluttered.

The Haves and the Have Nots
08/Mar/2019 07:13 AM

I had a meeting with a young filmmaker last night. He is planning to do a scripted short that he hopes to enter into film festivals in order to get his name out there. He asked me to come onboard as a producer/consultant. Though he is a fan my work, I, of course, declined the offer, feeling that the formalized structure that he hopes to employee is really not my forte. But, more than the meeting itself, going to this guy's house was truly the experience.

This guy lived in his parent's palatial mansion in the Bel Aire section of Los Angeles. It was a really nice house. There, he had a room set up that he called his Production Suite. In that suite he keeps some really high-end filmmaking equipment. The best cameras, tripods, sound and lighting equipment, you name it… The kind of equipment that most new filmmakers would only dream about possessing. But, there he was, he hadn't even made a film yet, didn't known how to use most of it, but he owned all of that equipment.

What will eventually come of his film and/or his filmmaking career, I cannot tell you. But, I will say, that when you come from a background such as that your chances of breaking through, in any arena in life, greatly increases.

All of this sent me to thinking back to my youth, my first girlfriend, and how I first encountered massive wealth. I am sure I have mentioned this in some piece of literature before but I was in the 7th grade. I lived in a rather junky one-bedroom apartment with my mother on 6th Street in the section of L.A. that later became known as Koreatown. Just a few blocks down the street from us began the Hancock Park District where there were and are a lot of opulent mansions. This is where my girlfriend lived. Her house was massive. It had a pool, a tennis and a basketball court. Though by my nature I have never been an envious person, I certainly did see the difference in our lifestyles. My mother and I didn't even own a car. She would get up every morning and take the bus downtown to work and I would either walk, hitchhike, or take the bus to school. Though I liked the girl a lot, and she seemed to like me, I could never expose my humble background to her or where I lived as I believed that would not only be very embarrassing but it would be the deal breaker.

It was really very similar when I went to high school. There were those of us who lived in apartments in the flatlands of Hollywood and there were those who were raised in their mansions in the hills. They always drove the best cars, if they were would-be musicians they had the best equipment, if they were would-be actors they had the best clothing, and so on... Then, there was the rest of us...

Again, this is simply a definition of life and how it was very clearly illustrated to me in my youth. It is not a judgment call.

But, the one thing that is clear is that when you come up in an environment of financial opulence your chances of achieving your dream greatly increases. This is the same when you grow up in an emotionally supportive family and so on. There is the have and then there is the people like me, the have nots.

I believe due to my upbringing, I have always gravitated towards the downtrodden and the less than savory. It has became my signature. I mean, I obviously didn't come from money. I never made very much money—though I have tried. Though where you come from does not have to be your ultimate definition in life, it certainly influences who you can and most probably will become.

If you come from money, you expect a certain lifestyle. If you come from money, you are breed into a world where there are other people with money. Thus, that is your peer group. Thus, those are the people you interact with and the people you take your inspiration and influences from. Just as those who come in on the lower levels of society associate with their own.

All this being said, there is really no perfect formula to move from being a have not to a have though many/most people attempt to do just that. Sure, a lot of people lie about who they are, what they have done, and what they have. Sure, a lot of people aspire to become more. Some even make it. But, who you are, who you were as a child, how you lived as a child will always be with you. It will always shape your vision, your emotions, your choices, and your decisions.

Hopefully you are a have. Then you live in a mansion, have a great car, and have all of this great brand new filmmaking equipment. If not, just give life your best shot. That's all I have done. I still never made it to a mansion with a pool and a tennis court but that's okay, I guess, I never really played tennis anyway and the chlorine in a pool always seems to give my blonde hair a tint of green. ☺

* * *

07/Mar/2019 08:08 AM

The truth is only known by those who lived it.

* * *

07/Mar/2019 08:07 AM

Just because you don't like something does not make it bad.

Just because you don't like someone does not make them bad.

Be more than your options.

The People That Take No Responsibility
07/Mar/2019 07:58 AM

As we pass through life I believe that each of us have encountered a person or persons that do something but take no responsibility for their actions. I am not speaking about a person who does a selfless action and does not want to be praised for their deed. I am speaking about someone who does some self-motivated something that hurts or damages the life of someone else but when they are confronted with this truth they deny any personal responsibility or have a justification for taking/making the action that they did.

Each person has a reason for doing what they do in life. One of the biggest reasons is money. People do all kinds of things to make money. But, think about how much life-damage has been created by someone who does what he or she does simply to make money. Look around at the pollution on this planet and the people who have suffered because of it while someone got paid to unleash that pollution. Did they care? No. They particularly did not care as long as they were healthy and wealthy and able to live well on the money they made that damaged the lives of others.

This mindset goes from the very small scale to the very large. Simply look at someone who smokes and the damage they are unleashing to this life-place because of their smoking, yet they have a million justifications for doing what they do, they have a million reasons why they do not care, and they have a million denials. They possess this logic until they are dying from lung cancer, a heart attack, or a stroke, and then their attitude of taking no responsibility changes to a mindset of blame—

blaming others, not themselves. And, this takes us to the heart of the problem; namely, personal psychology.

If a person lives in a space of taking no responsibility, that is who they are. You can tell them that they should care: care about other people, care about the people they may be hurting, care about the environment, care about whatever, but they will not listen. Who they are is a selfish, self-involved person, who does not have the ability to care about others; even though some pretend that they do. But, that is just a lie. Another selfish illusion that they project to the world to keep their bank account flush and their ego stroked.

I was watching a Ro. Co. Click Flick on TV last night and it was about this one girl who lied about who she truly was so she could snag this rich, attractive guy and marry him as she had no money and her life was a mess. Probably most of us won't personally encounter a life situation like that but think about all the lies that have been told within the bounds of a relationship; either to get a person, keep a person, or get rid of a person. Lies in life are abundant. But, does the person who is lying or altering the truth to suit their own perspective care about the impact of their lie on the life of one person or a million people? No. They just want what they want and a telling a lie is a way to get it. Have you ever lied to get what you want?

The fact is, people do what they do. Some people do very bad things. Some people do things that hurt other people. From a distance, most of us would say that is wrong. Yet, look how many supporters some of these people have. Simply look to politics or the entertainment industry—simply look to the corporate world. People do all kinds of bad things on all kinds of levels that hurt other people and hurt the world but they each have their own reason for doing what they do and most never take any responsibility for their actions, and in some cases they even develop fans by doing what they do.

Okay… Where does this leave us? Have you ever been hurt by the actions of someone else? Most of us have. What was the instigator of the pain? Was it an actual blow delivered by what some other person did or was it simply something that someone else did that you did not like? If someone did something that directly hurt you, there is one person who is to blame. On the other hand, if you just don't like what someone did, than maybe you can simply rethink your drink, change your pattern of thought and make lemonade out of lemons—turn it around to something positive.

All this being said, as conscious individuals, attempting to make all-things and every-body better, we must always keep ourselves free from hurting others based upon personal undefined desire or focused targeting. We must always consciously enter into each life situation, each personal interaction, and do what we do from the perspective of Pure Thought and Realization. We should never do something just because we can get away with. We should never do something intentionally trying to take a shot at or hurt someone. Mostly, we should never go into a space of denial and/or make excuses for our responsibility in creating any situation that did damage to the life of someone/anyone else.

As I always say, care enough to care. It is you who can make the world a better place. But, to do so, you must own your responsibility in all of your life actions.

* * *

06/Mar/2019 08:01 AM

Accomplishment happens when you decide to do something. But, this is also the place where karma is born.

Life is a balance between achieving and paying the price for your achievements.

* * *
05/Mar/2019 08:07 AM

Think about all of the times that you have eaten a piece of fruit that had seeds in it. Think about all of the times that you simply disposed of those seeds after you finished eating that piece of fruit. Think about how many trees may have grown if you would have planted those seeds instead of simply throwing them away. Positive change begins with what you decide to do.

The Emotion of Emotion
04/Mar/2019 08:22 AM

Life is an emotionally driven process. You feel, thereby you live. You feel, thereby you do.

Some people are more emotional than others. Some people are very emotional about their emotions. This, while some people are very subdued in their emotions. They control them, they hide them, and/or they do not broadcast them. Which one are you?

Every person feels their emotions on a personal level. But, the mistake that many/most people make is that they do not comprehend the concept that the emotions they feel is not necessary the emotions that someone else is feeling. Here is where many of the world's interpersonal problems are given birth to—one person feeling one thing while the other person feels something totally different.

Have you ever observed; watched as someone attempts to make another person feel a specific way—a way that they may not actually feel? In some cases, due to the exuberance of that person's emotions they do pull others into their way of feeling, at least for a moment. Here is where all kinds of life regret are given birth to.

Then, there is one person feeling an emotion and attempting to loudly broadcast that feeling to others. This method works much better in many cases because people with like mind will listen. But, is one person's emotions worthy of begin felt by one or a million others? Isn't that just mindless mind control? Yet, this happens all the time. How about with you? Where do you find yourself in this equation? Do you fall prey to the emotions of someone else? Have you fallen prey to the emotions of someone else?

Next, there is the harboring of emotions from afar. …One person feeling someway about someone else when the other person does not feel that same emotion. This is where fantasy is born but it is also where life damage is born because that one emotion-based person is seeking a desired end-goal from someone else with a completely different set of emotions.

Maybe a person has his or her eyes set on someone else in the form of love, lust, or control. Thus, they act on that emotion and attempt to find favor with the person by evoking that same emotion in them. If you think back to the '80s pop song, *Jessie's Girl,* by Rick Springfield, there is a perfect example. One man falls in love with someone else's girlfriend and desires to win her over. Though this is not an uncommon scenario, and takes place to varying degrees all the time, is it healthy? No, it is not. It is simply one person being controlled by their emotions and following an unhealthy, unhelpful path guided by their emotions.

There is also the emotion of anger. This is obviously one of the most destructive emotions in the human emotional vocabulary.

Think about a time when you were angry. What made you angry? Most likely it was somebody doing something that you did not like. But, did you ever ponder this fact while you were angry? Probably not. You were just raging with emotion. You felt what you felt. You didn't like or care what that other person felt and that was that.

Who was right and who was wrong? It was two people doing two things based upon their emotions. When we break it down we can most possibly point the finger at the initial instigator as the culprit, yet one person did one thing, one person reacted to that one thing, and a whole course of life-actions based upon emotions were set into motion. Equally what? Most probably, life damage.

So, who are you and what do you feel? What have your emotions caused you to do? What do your emotions cause you to do? Do you control them or do you allow them to control you?

One can say that a person who keeps their emotions in check is a more evolved individual. Yes, that is true. But, there is still the person next door emotionally screaming at the top of their lungs damaging the life of all those within earshot. What can you do?

Life is an emotion-based process. Who you are and what you will ultimately become will be defined by your emotions and how you react to them. Are you going to let your emotions lead you down a pathway that hurts you and others? Are you going to allow your emotions to lead you down a pathway where you legacy is defined by your emotions? Or, can you be in control? Can you be more than your emotions? Think about it.

* * *

03/Mar/2019 04:47 PM

"Who's life have I hurt and what can I do to fix the damage?" If this is not the first question you ask yourself every morning you are destine to live a life defined by karmic upheaval.

*   *   *

03/Mar/2019 08:07 AM

Question the answer.

What Do You Think About?
28/Feb/2019 07:13 AM

When you are sitting around doing nothing, what do you think about? When you are waiting in an office for an appointment, what do you think about? When you are going to sleep at night, what do your think about? When you wake up in the morning before your alarm goes off, what do you think about?

Most people have a very random traveling of constant thoughts. Their thoughts go from one onto the next onto the next. They don't think about what they think about. How about you?

Certainly, at the heart of meditation is the controlling and the hoped for stopping of thoughts. But, that is an advanced exercise that very few people choose to attempt to perform. Mostly, most people, allow their thoughts to race from one to the next to the next.

Like the old saying goes, *"You are what you eat."* Even more defining is, *"You are what you think."* Our thoughts cause each of us to behave in a certain manner. Our thoughts cause us to take action. Our thoughts drive us to action. Our thoughts cause us to be happy, sad, angry, or passive.

What do your thoughts cause you to think and feel? What do your thought cause you to do? And, do you ever think about this or do you simply allow your thoughts to control you?

Your life and what you do with your life is defined by your thoughts. You think about what you have lived and what you have lived through. You think about what you want to bring into your life. You fantasize. But, all of this is locked into your mind until your thoughts cause you to take action. Then, once this action has been taken, your thoughts are about what is taking place around you, guided by your experiences that happened due to your thoughts.

We all want something in life. We all want to do something with our life. For some, they never actualize what they want—moving it from their mind to their physical reality. For others, what they visualize in their mind causes them to act and, in some cases, that actions cause damage and harm to themselves and to others. Then what?

One of the main components of reality to keep in mind is, simply because you desire something does not mean that another person desires the same thing. In your mind, in your thoughts, in your fantasies, everything works out to a personal perfection but life is not like that. People are different people. What is locked in the thoughts of one person's mind is not the same as what is being thought in another person's mind. Some understand this reality others do not. Thus, thoughts thought by one may cause a reality shift to many.

Your thoughts are your thoughts. That's fine. That's human reality. But, the moment your thoughts bring you to take action, then your thoughts are projected outwards and they affect others. This is where good things are born; this is also where bad things are given birth to.

The conscious person always questions, *"Why am I thinking what I am thinking?"* Why are you thinking what you are thinking? What are your thought causing you to do? Are your actions based on your thoughts affecting anyone else? If so, what does that action, based upon your thoughts, mean to the life of that person?

To live a good and a conscious life you need to ponder these questions while you are thinking. You thoughts equal your actions, equaling the thoughtful reaction of others. How are your thoughts affecting you? How are your thoughts affecting others? And, do your thoughts allow you to care about what you thoughts have caused you to do to you, to others, and to life in general?

When Is It Too Late?
25/Feb/2019 07:41 AM

As we pass through life we each develop mannerism. We each develop the way that we encounter life, people, and situations. From these factors we set a course of events into motion in our life. From these factors we set our ultimate destiny into motion. We do what we do based upon these factors.

How many people take the time to study who they are and why they do the things that they do? Yes, most people know what they want. Yes, they know what they hope to achieve. But, how many study why they want what they want, why they do what they do to achieve what they want, and why they behave towards others in the manner that they do? Most people simply react as they live their life.

One of the interesting things about age is that you get to view people and life through the perspective of time. You get to see who a person was then, hear what they hoped to become, witness the way they behaved towards others and towards life, view what they did to achieve their goals, and view what they have finally became. From an outside perspective, and through the window of time, you can truly see how and why people have ended up where they have ended up.

In some case, where a person ends up is a good and positive thing. They set a goal for themselves and their family, were focused and kind to others, and they arrived at their goal. In other cases, people where angry, dishonest, wasteful, imprudent, promiscuous, mean spirited, hurtful of others, dismissive, power trippers, and/or isolationists. From this they too ended up where one could have predicated. But, you could not/cannot tell them where their path would lead. They only knew it when they reached the end of their path. Then, they found themselves lonely, alone, isolated, broke, or hated.

Have you ever watched a hoarder pass through their lifetime? They have a million reasons/excuses for collecting and acquiring all of the stuff that they obtain but all that happens is that their life and the life of those around them becomes completely controlled by all of the stuff that they cannot relinquish. They live is a trash-ridden hell. That is just one very obvious example but look at the way people interact with life. Look at the way people treat other people. Each person has a specific method for doing so. Look at the help they provide and then look at the damage they create. Do they ever change? In most cases, no. They develop a path, follow that path, never mentally governor that path, and that path controls all of their life interactions which ultimately defines who they become giving birth to the final definition of their entire life.

In youth, there is the sense that there is always tomorrow. If you don't have it today, you will get it tomorrow. There is also the sense that people be dammed. There are a lot of fish in the sea, as the old saying goes, and if you have walk over a few people to obtain whatever it is you desire, that is just the way it is. But, is it? Is that the truth of life or is that simple a false ideology that has been programmed into the minds of the masses. Think about it, if you hurt somebody in your progression towards your own defined end goal that hurt remains forever in the mind of the person you hurt.

Thus, what do you believe will be the ultimate ramifications of that hurtful action in your ultimate life definition?

People always find excuses for doing what they do. But, today is not tomorrow. And, it is tomorrow that holds your ultimate destiny.

People end up alone. People end up broke. People end up shamed. People end up shunned. But, who sets all of that into motion. Most likely, it was the person themselves.

So, here is the question, when is it too late? When is it too late to change who you have decided that you are and what you have become. And, are you strong enough to make the choice to change who you are and are you powerful enough to control your mind to the degree where you can actually make that change?

Wherever you find yourself in life, that is where you are—that is who you are. But, where you are today is not where you will end up tomorrow. Never fall into the illusion that what you have today: how you look, how you feel, what you possess will be there tomorrow. What you live today, how you live today, what you do today to yourself and to others will define where you will end up tomorrow.

You may not be able to see where you will end up. But, you can study your actions and your behavior and have an educated guess. Who will you be at the end of your days and how are you going to control that outcome right now?

* * *

24/Feb/2019 08:39 AM

The next time you encounter somebody saying or doing something negative, override their actions by saying or doing something positive. Observe the response.

The next time you are thinking something negative about a person, take control of your mind and think something positive about the person. Observe the response.

The next time you are about to do something negative to a person, stop yourself and do something positive. Observe the response.

* * *

24/Feb/2019 08:37 AM

It is very simple, in life negativity breeds negativity. Yet, when negativity finds the person who instigated the negativity they always question, *"Why me?"*

Isn't it better to only say and do positive things?

The Last Time It Snowed in L.A.
22/Feb/2019 02:10 PM

I was listening to the radio yesterday as I was driving and the newscaster mentioned that the last time it snowed in L.A. was January of 1962. This provided an answer for me as my lady had just asked me the question the night before, *"When was the first time I saw it snow?"* The reason she asked was that we were watching the news and a family from Florida was passing through So. Cal. and they encountered snow for the first time in all of their lives. It wasn't in L.A. but it was in some nearby community.

This has been a very cold and rainy winter here in L.A. Sure, sure, I know a lot of places have been a lot colder and a lot weter. But, it has been noticeable.

It does snow in the mountains around L.A. and occasionally in some of the places around the area with higher elevations; like it did yesterday. But, I guess '62 was the last time in actually snowed in L.A. ...I would have been four.

I remember the day it snowed in L.A. very well. My mother, father, and I went out onto the front lawn of our house on Santa Barbara Avenue, which later became Martin Luther King, Jr. Boulevard, and felt the snow falling down. It wasn't a lot of snow or anything but for a four year old it was quite an experience.

One of the main things that you really need to keep in mind as you pass through life is, you really need to embrace the experiences you are experiencing. I mean, they may not be as monumental as encountering the last time in snowed in L.A., over fifty years ago, but each experience is unique to you. You should really take the time to live it, feel it, and know it so you can remember it. Because in life—your life, those experiences are all you really have.

* * *
22/Feb/2019 01:50 PM

If you are willing to take anything you will always find something.

* * *
21/Feb/2019 07:47 AM

You can help or you can hurt there really is no in-between.

When You Think You're Helping But You're Actually Hurting
20/Feb/2019 09:14 AM

Have you ever been in a situation where you thought your were doing something to help a person but you were later told by the person that what you did actually hurt them? Why did this happen? Why did your appraisal of the situation differ from the person you were trying to help? The answer to this is very simply; you are not that other person. You are you. You are not them. Thus, no matter how much you project your own life understanding about personal needs, personal wants, and what is or is not help onto someone else, you can never understand what another person is actually wanting, feeling, desiring, or what they actually needs.

Many of the world's problems, especially on the interpersonal level, are giving birth to by one person thinking that they know what another person wants or needs. Again, this goes back to the mind of one person believing that they have the answer(s) for another. But, this is never the case. If a person asks you for something specific and you give it to them, then if they later decide that gift was a mistake, it is on them. But, if you instigate the giving, what you give may be exactly what they do not want or need.

Think about your own life. Maybe it was in your childhood or maybe it was in your adulthood, how many times has someone made a decision for you and that decision was totally against what you believed? Maybe you were given something. Maybe your were not given what you thought you needed. Maybe somebody did something that they believed was right for you. Maybe somebody did something that they believed was what you needed. But, what happened next was the exact opposite. Why did this situation occur? Because someone believed they knew you and decided they knew what was right for you. But, who knows anybody? If what you need is not allowed to be expressed, if someone decided what you need, what you should want, or what is right for you then that decision is based in his or her mind and not yours. Your mind is never theirs. Thus, how can they know anything about you?

The answer to all of this? Leave other people alone. Never assume you know what they want, what they need, or how they should feel. Then, all people are allowed to be who they are and live the life they were destine to live defined by their own perception or reality.

Karma Consciousness or the Consciousness of Karma
20/Feb/2019 07:23 AM

You have done something that has hurt someone but instead of understanding the pain you have inflicted you think about yourself.

You have taken something from someone but instead of understanding the loss you have created in the life of that other person you think about yourself.

You have lied to someone but instead of understanding the confusion and chaos your expressed falsehood has created in the life of that other person you only think about yourself.

You have spread rumors behind the back of someone but instead of caring about the damage you have done to the reputation of that person you only think about yourself.

If you ask anyone why they have done what they have done that has hurt or altered the life of another person they will always provide you with a reason for what they have done. But, is that reason the truth? Though it may the truth that projects from their own mind, their mind only thinks about themselves. Their mind is only concerned with themselves. Ask the person who was affected in a negative manner by what another person has done and they will have a completely different perspective. Whose perspective is the correct perspective and based in the absolute truth?

There are always two sides to any interpersonal equation. There is the person who is the instigator/the doer and there is the person who is on the receiving end. The moment that doer sets a course of events into motion that hurts another person in any manner they become the criminal but how many people think of themselves as a criminal. They may think of themselves as the victor. They may think of themselves as the winner. They may think of themselves as the controller. But, they never think of the other person as anything more than the adversary, the diminished, or the one they have conquered.

People raise themselves into life defined by a desire to become. People raise themselves into life defined by a desire to have. Ask yourself, what is becoming? What is having? What is any accomplishment or win in life defined by if that personally defined achievement takes from the life of someone else? But, who thinks about this? Who thinks about their impact? Who cares about their impact? Who cares about anything or anybody as long as they have gotten what they want?

Have you ever observed a person who is at the top of their game? Have you ever watched a person who is at the top of their profession? Have you ever watched a person who is flush with cash? What do you observe? Is the person caring or giving? Is the person extremely conscious of those they have climbed over to get to the top? Is the person cognizant of what they have done to get where they are? Or, do they only relish in their own power and become very angry when someone challenges that power? And, if someone does, what does that person do to that person? Do they care about them? Do they understand them? Do they give to them? Or, do they find a way to attempt to diminish that individual?

Observe a person who has done something that has hurt someone else. Now, observe that same person when something is done to them. Who do they think about? Do they think about the person or people they have hurt? Or, does all focus shift only to themselves as they blame the person who has counter attacked?

Most people never think about the pain that they caused other people. People never think abut the karma they are creating. People are selfish. Why do you think there is so much chaos in the world? Why do you think there is so much pain in the world? Why do you think there is so much conflict in the world? The answer, people only care about themselves. Thus, giving birth to a never-ending stream of karma.

If you want to know who a person truly is, observe how they think about, talk about, and treat other people. If you want to know who you truly are, observe how you think about, talk about, and treat other people. Who are they? Who are you? And, do they/do you treat people the way they should be treated?

If you want to see where your life will end up. Study the way you interact with other people. Observe they way you speak about, think about, and treat other people. You define them as they will ultimately define you. You set your own destiny into motion. Be the source of caring.

* * *
20/Feb/2019 07:23 AM

Is a person's judgment of another person ever correct?

* * *
20/Feb/2019 07:21 AM

Always question who is saying what and why.

Violence for No Reason
19/Feb/2019 08:44 AM

I was walking down *State Street* in Santa Barbara the other day and there were a couple of Caucasian homeless men sitting on the sidewalk. Nothing unusual about that. Then, up walks another homeless guy, African-American, and starts harassing one of the men sitting on the sidewalk. I'm guessing it was over the fact that the guy sitting down had one of those Styrofoam containers holding what looked to be a bunch of *Chicken McNuggets* that someone had obviously bought him. The man stood there in all of his aggressive posturing, telling the guy he was going to kick his ass and kept doing one of those things where he cocks his arm back and pretends to launch a punch. The guy sitting down finally said, *"Go ahead and do it then."*

The night before all of this I was watching the TV show *Ridiculousness* and Rob asked Sterling and Channel if they saw a fight would they intercede? Which all kind of set me to thinking as I was watching this situation unfold.

The fact is, it was kind of funny the stance the guy was in as he threatened the seated man. His legs were wide open as he stood over the guy. It sent me to thinking back to my youth when a guy was standing like that and one of my friends went and kick him in the nuts from behind. The guy being kicked obviously tumbled to the ground in pain. It would have been so easy for me to do that or to do so many other things to protect the guy. But, then what? All my actions would have equaled was layering violence upon violence. Certainly, if it was a child or a woman being threatened I would have stepped in. But, all that would have happened if I kicked that guy's ass was that I would probably end up in jail. Both of them would still be homeless, waiting for the occurrence of the next day, nothing in their or my life would be any better, and who knows what would happen next. I would have solved nothing. So, I let it go…

All this, while numerous people walked by and did not even take notice. This provides you with a clear window into the mind of society.

I've witness a lot of violence in my life. I've also interacted with my fair share. But, what does any of it ever prove? Sure, the people who instigate it always seem to have a reason—they always seem to have a justification. But, reasons and justifications are only in the mind of the individual. They are rarely held by the greater whole. And, if they are, they most likely have been programmed to hold a specific belief about a specific thing.

The fact is, there is violence all around us. What can we do? Do we walk down the street and ignore it? Do we jump in and add violence to violence? I don't know? There is no cure. No matter how enlightened we claim modern society has become, nothing has changed. There are still people attempting to overpower others by whatever means they have available. Sad but true. I will say, all violence ever equals is more violence and the hurting of the life of everyone involved. They may not see it then. They may feel dominant and powerful. But power fades. Dominance is an illusion. And, who you hurt to today sets the stage for you being hurt tomorrow.

There is no absolute answer. But, the one thing that is for certain is that violence is never a good thing.

Nudity, Political Correctness, and the What's What of the What's Now
18/Feb/2019 07:41 AM

Sometimes I am asked why don't I have any photographs of nude females in association with the production still I have on my website in regard to my films as some (but not all) of my films have seminude or nude females in them. Like many things in life, the answer to that question is a bit complicated. But, in essence, long ago I decided not to show nudity on the site as not only did it put some people off but it then put a label on my site and myself.

To know me, I am not and have never been into porn. I just never really liked it. There are a million reasons for that, I guess, but that's the fact of the fact. Paintings and artistic photographs of nude females, however, I always found those beautiful and appealing. I guess, it's an art thing verses just a sex thing.

If you watch my films, you will see that for the most part any nudity in them is solely there for the sake of nudity. Meaning, there is no reason for it. It simply occurs. It does not lead to sex or anything like that. It is just there to artistic frame the female form in the realms of cinematic art. In some cases, the art in my mind has been better represented on the screen than at other times. But, any nudity in any of my films has always been designed with art and appreciation for the female form as the central ideology.

Sure, sure, some may question, *"Why no male nudity?"* I'm just not into that. I don't see the beauty. Sure, some do, but I don't. Thus, that never finds its way into my films.

All this being said, we have slowly but surely entered into a time period of enhanced political correctness. Right now, it seems that everyone is seeking to find a new and highly defined sense of what is right and what is wrong—who is right and who is wrong. There is a lot of anger out there and that anger is seeking a target. For the most part, a lot of it has been focused on men, what they have done in the past, and the entire male mindset. Certainly, this trend will continue, at least for a time, as all large scale trends tend to do. It will define what is now and possibly what comes next. There's nothing wrong with this as this is just the way life is.

Due to this current and pervasive mindset, however, falling by the wayside is the one time expression of exploitation cinema. Not porn, for I imagine that will forever have an audience. But, the cinema of doing what you do for only reason(s) brewed up in the mind of the artistic filmmaker. Though I certainty never considered myself a creator of exploitation cinema, there have always been those people out there who want to cast their own judgment on the creation of others. But, like I often say, they were not the creator, they were not there when the creation was being created, they were not part of the team that created the creation, so how can they truly know anything about the process of the creation? Theirs is only speculation at best.

In any case, for those of you who have wondered, that is the answer.

Sometimes art is better left to those who seek out the art and fully immerse themselves in that art. Sometimes, you can't just paint your art on the walls for everyone to see because the majority of the people who happen upon it simply will not understand it.

Reach Out a Hand of Friendship
16/Feb/2019 07:32 AM

There is a lot of confrontation in the world. I frequently speak about this subject because this is one of the most complicated conditions we must each formulate a conclusion about as we individually pass through our lives. But, what is the source of much of this confrontation? It is one person doing something that another person does not like which leads to all kinds of havoc. Maybe this is on a very small scale of one person doing one thing to one person. Or, it may be on a larger scale where one person does something that actually hurts the life evolution of another person. But, the equation is always the same; someone does not like what another person has done.

Let's think about this for a moment. What if that one person had not done what they had done? Everything in both people's life would be different; probably better. Yet, it was done.

Now, this takes us to the next step in this calculation. Since the person did it, they felt they had the right to do it. Maybe it was done by accident or maybe it was done intentionally but, none-the-less, it was done. Thus, one person did it and one person was affected by it. From this, conflict was born.

Think about your own life. Think about the people you have become mad at. What did they do that made you mad? Now, question what was your involvement in the situation? Did you instigate it? Did you create it? Did you participate in it? Or, were you simply a victim?

Now, think about the people who have become mad at you. What did you do to them that made them angry? Moreover, did you care that they were angry with you? Or, did you not care at all?

Once conflict is born, some people take the high road, try to understand the other person's feelings, ask for forgiveness, and try to fix any damage they instigated. But, few people are like that. Most, simply either do not care at all or lie and deny about any personal involvement in the situation.

But, all any of this equals is Mind Stuff. It equals one person being hurt. One person doing the hurting. One person left victimized. One person left triumphant. One person seeking revenge.

All of this is not good! It is not good for the person. It is not good for the friends and family of these people. It is not good for the life of the people involved. It is not good for the people witnessing the situation as they are forced to take sides. It is not good for the greater everything.

So, what can you do? Reach out a hand a friendship. Care about the other person. If you are on the instigating end, put your ego in check and try to remove the damage you instigated. If you are on the receiving end, forgive. Mostly, never expect the other person to be the first person to instigate doing anything. Be the first one to attempt to make things right.

Think about it… All people are better/greater as a team instead of advisories. Reach out a hand a friendship. Quash conflict. Say you're sorry. Forgive. Make the world a better place.

The Unity of Unity Verse the Conflict of Conflict
15/Feb/2019 08:24 AM

Life is broken down into two very distinct categories of interpersonal contact. Their definitions could be described as unity verses conflict. Unity causes a coming together of helpful interaction whereas conflict leads to the disassembling of all things good and positive. If you look at your life, if you look at what you have lived while living your life, if you look to yourself and the way you have behave towards others, you will understand what occurs from each of these two life defining sets of human behaviors. Thus, it is easy to view how these opposites defined not only the life that you have live but also the life that was experienced by all others who have interacted with you.

To begin, let's take a look at the mindset of unity. This is where people come together and form a greater whole; supposedly causing betterment for all those involved.

Unity occurs for many reasons but it is essential to note that not all of them are positive. People congregate for many purposes, guided by their own inner personal motivations. As anger or motivated hatred for a person or a cause is very invigorating, many a group of people have come together as one unit to fight what they feel is wrong. But, anger is never a positive motivator, just as what occurs, based in anger, never leads to the gateway of a greater good. But, look to your own life; whether it was the team you were on, the political party you subscribed to, the church you belong to, the sport's team you root for, the race of people you were born into, or the person or situation you hated, think how many times you have encountered a condition where people congregated based solely on wanting to win. They came together as a means to prove their superiority. Now, think about this, have you ever been on the receiving end of a group of people who were mad at you or did not like what you stood for? How did that feel? Thus, unity forms an army. But armies, more often than not, only create hurt and havoc.

Positive unity comes from a somewhat different mental perspective. It comes from a place of a foundational understanding of two or more people walking a similar path. But, this too is a complicated scenario. For example, in the 1960s and the 1970s if a man had long hair they were all identified as being of the same cult. As up until that point in modern Western history, a man with long hair was not the norm. From this, if a person saw another man with long hair there was an instant unity. But, this also came with a price tag, as there was a much larger group of people who hated anyone who had stepped away from the norm and had grown their hair.

In my own case, though I certainly understood this mindset, by the time I was in my mid adolescents, I saw the flaw in this immediate unity solely based upon outward appearance. Sure, that other guy had long hair like I did, but we were more than likely very different people. Many of the men with long hair smoked, did drugs and the like. Me, I was on the path of spiritual realization and natural living, guided by teachers from the East. Thus, though we may have appeared similar to the outside masses, we had very different motivations for why we were part of the counterculture.

Perhaps, this was ideally demonstrated when I was in my early twenties and going to grad school.

I had taken a small flat in Manhattan Beach. My classes were in the evening that day so I though I would take a walk on the beach. I was crossing the street when I young man in a car, with short hair, jams past me and yells, *"Get a job!"* He did that simply because of my appearance and my being free during the day. But, I did have a job. I played music. I taught the martial arts and yoga. I was just not doing it right then. So, this leads us to a deeper understanding of though outward appearances and inwards motivations causes a person to appear in a certain manner, the outward projections of that mindset is not an ideal representation of who a person wholly is. And, from this, though a person may appear to be one thing, in actually they are actually something very different.

This takes us to the inner motivations of a person and why, though this inner motivation may cause a person to form a bond of unity with someone else, that unity may not be substantial enough to cause people to remain as a cohesive whole.

Certainly, outward appearances are a very small percentage of what brings people together. More often than not, people come together based upon a specific frame of mind. But, the ultimate question always has to be asked, *"Why does a person believe what they believe?"*

Belief is one of the hardest concepts to understand when charting the reality of human existence. Most beliefs are programmed into us. Our culture, our family, and our friends drive them into our minds. Then, there is our life experience(s). We are created by the way we are treaded by others. We are guided in how we react by the way we were treated. From this, some people rise to great heights while others are left lost in the masses. But, think about this, you were created, you lived what you lived, you did what you did based upon what you lived, you interacted with others based upon how you were taught to react, but, do you still love whom you loved yesterday? Do you still love what you loved yesterday? Are you still the same person, doing the same thing(s), that you did yesterday? Almost universally, the answer to these questions is that you have changed. Yet, you are still defined by who and what you once loved and what you once did based upon the feelings you felt then.

You did what you did for a reason. You did it to find unity and sustenance. You did it because you felt that was who you are. You did it because you wanted to become a something. You did it because you wanted to be more. But, how did that more affect the everything else? How did that more affect they anyone else? You did what you did because you wanted to do it. You did what you did because you thought it would equal a desired end. You did what you did either to join a group of the greater whole or to create a group of believers that followed you into the greater whole. Ultimately, you did what you did because you were only thinking about you. Thus, though you joined a group to do what you did, you formed a group to do what you desired, it was ultimately only you doing desiring an end result which caused you to do what you do and, thus, though you sought a unity to achieve this end, there was only a fragmented unity of several or more people setting about on a course that most likely only helped themselves. So, where is unity? It is only one person doing one thing that helps themselves so there is no unity at all.

This is why there is the dichotomy of unity verse conflict. Why is there unity? To gain a desired end. Why is their conflict? Because people's desired ends are different. They may want the same thing right now, but they will want something very different tomorrow. This is why groups shatter. This is why friendships shatter. This is why couples break up.

Ultimately, a unity is only as strong as the people who form that unity. Ultimately, a unity is only as strong as the length of time people share the same desired end.

Thus, most unity always equals conflict. Because the unity caused conflict with those who are not part of the group and as the unity will ultimately dissolve is causes interpersonal conflict because once one person changes their mind, everything in the group changes.

Know why you seek unity. Understand your reasoning. And, know unity is only a strong as its weakest link.

I Guess I'm the Only Person in Hollywood Who Isn't Hungry
13/Feb/2019 05:58 PM

Kinda funny... I had a meeting with an agent today. A meeting I walked out on.

To tell the story... I had split ways with my most recent agent a couple of months ago. It wasn't that he was a bad guy or anything; it was just that people and their business mannerism change over time. I'd been with him about ten years. Once upon a time he worked hard for me. But, those times are gone. So, I was gone.

I've never really had a good relationship with agents throughout my career. Mt first agent was great. She was very nice, professional, and hooked me into a lot of gigs. But, then she retired. After that, I've had a few different agents. It's not that agents are bad people, it's simple a weird mindset that they possess making money by getting their percentage from their clients. Most of the female agents are failed actresses. Most of the male agents have this weird hustler mindset.

Anyway... I showed up for the meeting today. The receptionist was very nice, told me that the main agent was on the phone upstairs and I should sit down and wait. Which I happily did. Up walks the sub-agent, *"Scott?"* *"That's me."* She hands me one of those basic fill out your info papers. She inquires, *"Did I bring a headshot?"* *"No,"* I answered, *"This is the digital world. But, I have a million online."* She replies with a smirk, *"We like headshots."* To ease the tension I smiling said, *"Oh, you're old school."* But I did not like her condescending vibe. As I filled out the info paper I could not help but think about all of the bad reviews this agency had gotten that I had read online. But, you know, everybody has their own internal motivations for what they say, especially anonymously online, so I never pay those kind of things too much mind. I like to define the world by my own experiences.

Filled out, I stood up and handed her the info paper. She immediately handed me some Sides. For those of you who don't know, Sides are where the dialogue for a scene is written that the actors recite.

I don't know what it was... Her attitude??? But, the fact is, agents never ask you to Read (audition for them), they sign you by your face, who you are in the industry, and your personality. I have never read for an agent! Initially, I took the Side but everything in my brain said, *"No way."* I turned around, laid the Sides down on her desk and said, *"You don't know who I am, do you? I don't Read, people hire me for who I am. I haven't Read for any one in over five years."*

The look on her face was priceless. She was one of those people with really expressive facial expressions. She was lost somewhere between anger and disbelief that someone would blow her off like that. I smiled. I gave her a *pranam* (prayer hands) and said, *"Thank you very much for your time."* I left. I'm just not that hungry.

Now, I am sure no actor has every done that to her. I mean all actors love to act. They want to prove they have their chops. Me, I don't care about any of that bullshit. Put me on a set and let me do my stuff. Or not. I don't care. Mostly, I was very surprised that this agent did not take the time to even investigate who I was/am before they brought me in. My philosophy always has been, know who you are dealing with before you deal with them. But, they obviously didn't do that. I mean, how could they represent me if they don't even know who I am and/or what I'm about?

Anyway, it was a good lesson learned. Another note in my book about the mindset of Hollywood agents and life. The thing is, people don't hire me via auditions. They offer me roles, (most of which I turn down), or they hire me for who I am. I think this agent lost out on a good opportunity with someone they didn't need to market but simply represent. But hey, that's Hollywood.

Starting the Fight Verses Fighting the Fight Verses Non-Fighting the Fight
12/Feb/2019 01:57 PM

I forever find it curious the way people attack other people from afar. Maybe it is talking behind their back, maybe it is saying negative things on the internet, maybe it is punching them in the back of the head when they had no way to see the attack coming. Why do people find it necessary to do this? First of all, why do people want to focus on the life of someone else and attack him or her in the first place? Whatever the answer, they, none-the-less, do.

The other thing I forever find curious is the way people, who once were the secret attackers, behave when they are attacked or when they do not like the actions that others have taken towards them. Again, we find them acting and reacting to the action(s) of others but now they do so from, as I like to call it, an offensive/defensive posture. They are again attacking and attempting to cause damage but now they blame their need for attack on someone else's instigation.

It is very easy to understand that if you live your life from a perspective of confrontation—if you live your life based upon taking actions that hurt someone else, no matter what your logic for doing so, you are going to encountering those who not only support you when you are attacking but those who are going to attack you because that is the mindset you embrace.

For most people, they do not want confrontation. They want to live their life as best as they can, doing what they do to find a means of surviving, without having to deal with the attacking protocols initiated by someone else. All you have to do is to look to your own life and ask yourself, *"Do I want to be attacked?"* The answer will most obviously be, *"No."* Though this is the case with virtually everyone, there are those who seek to cause another person pain. This desire can be based in all kinds of psychologically motivated ideologies that emulate solely from the mind of one person but hurt only equals hurt and it only opens the door for others to hurt the person who initially caused the hurt. And, pain is never fun.

We can all agree that people should do nothing to instigate pain: emotional, physical, or otherwise, to someone else. But, just look to all those who congregate around those who do unleash the pain. Look at all of the followers and supporters they develop. They possess them at least for a little while until they too fall from favor; most commonly due to the attack instigated by someone from far— someone unseen and unknown, someone who changes the way that person is perceived.

At the heart of hurting anyone is not realizing or not caring about the fact that each person is a human being. A human being that must find a way through their existence just as everyone else, including the attacker. With each attack, that existence is harder to chart out and realize, however, because their life has become damaged.

Now, the attacker may not care about this fact. They may not care about it until they are attacked, which, as life has proven, will sooner or later come to be a reality. Even then, however, they are not looking to the attacks they have unleashed as the causation factor. They are simply looking to the pain that they now feel.

Do you ever watch as an attacker attacks someone? Do you ever witness as they grow strong in the power that they feel? Why do you think they do it? They do it to be enchased by that sense of power. ...Power over the person they are attacking. Is this the way life should be live? No, of course not. But, look out to reality, look to all the people who hurt other people, are they the one's suffering? No, at least not at the original instigation of the attack. But, once they are the one under attack, then all blame shifts from themselves. They never look to the actions they initially took that created a world of hurt, pain, and suffering.

So, what are you going to do with all this? How are you going to live your life? Are you only going to think about you? Are you going to attack from afar and never fix the damage you have unleashed? Are you never going to care about the people you have hurt? Are you only going to think about yourself when you are hurt?

Life is complex. Life is complicated. But, the one thing that life should not be is a fight. You should not instigate situations where people are hurt.

Why can't you just do and say good thing? Say them about the people you love. Say them about the people you hate.

If you've done something that has hurt someone else, why can't you be strong enough to say, *"Sorry,"* and try to fix it?

Living a good life is really simple to understand. Don't attack. Don't hurt. Don't fight. Care about other people before you attempt to make a name for yourself via the instigation of pain. Really, it's just common sense.

*   *   *

12/Feb/2019 08:43 AM

If you are saying anything bad about anybody that means that person is in control of your thoughts and your words.

The 70s Were Great But They Ain't Ever Comin' Back AKA You Make What You Can With What You Have
12/Feb/2019 07:01 AM

I was kicking around in the late night, last night, flipping channels, and I noticed that the film, Jackie Brown was just beginning. I hadn't watched the entire film in a number of years so I sat back with a couple bottles of the grape and settled into the cinema. Good movie.

As is the case with many a Tarantino film, the 70s are heavily referenced. The 70s were a great era for film and music. This was especially the case for independent cinema. There was some really revolutionary stuff accomplished. Tarantino, who is just a years or so younger than me, grew up in that same era and he often makes reference to the 70s in his films. Me too... Of course, due to budgetary constraints, certainly not on the level of his films. *Jackie Brown* is an ideal example.

And, that's the thing; you do what you do with what you have...

Certainly, I have my share of fans of *Zen Cinema*. I also have my detractors, who always seem to be way more vocal. But, like I often say, *"Let's see you do what I have done. Make a film with the scope of my Zen Films for a budget of $300.00 (or less)."* Because that was/is my formalized budget. Sure, it can be done. I did it. But, do you have what it takes to get it done?

As the years went on my focus in cinema changed. For those of you who know me or know about me, about ten years ago I stopped doing narrative films and shifted my focus to *Pure*

Cinema. Cinema for the sake of cinema. No dialogue; characters but characters in their natural state. With visuals as the driving force.

Though many/most of the people who discuss my films speak of those I did before this point in my cinematic evolution, it is essential to note that they did not even start talking until I stopped making—making narrative films. So, what does what they have to say, say about anything?

This being said, it is essential to note that there was not a big, fast, and/or immediate break in my filmmaking style. I was doing non-narrative films long before that point in my cinematic evolution. It was simply that they were not as widely viewed as my other cinematic works.

All this being said, I am often asked what would cause me to do another traditional film? …Well, at least traditional in my sense of the word… ☺

I thought about this last night as I was watching *Jackie Brown*. One of the things would be to be able to make that 70s style film with actors from that era like Tarantino accomplished. But, the sad fact is, they are all so old now, if they are even still alive. So many of them are gone. Though the cinema of that era will live on forever. The people who created the cinematic art of that era are rapidly waning. Thus, the talent pool is forever diminishing and will soon be eternally lost.

I guess this is like life. There are those who do what they do, done in an era. There are those who rise up in that era and are forever defined by that era but then life is gone. We all get old. We all die. There are forever those who will discuss what others have done. But, they are not the doers. They are not the knowers. They are not the livers. They are not the creators. They are simply the talkers. But, once it is gone, it is gone. The life, the people, the era. So, all we can do is what we can do. All we can do is make what we make defined by what we have available to us in whatever era we live.

If You're Not Living the Zen You Shouldn't Be Talking About the Zen
11/Feb/2019 05:52 PM

Life is about experience. Life is about living your experience. Life is about embracing the truth as you know it. Life is about learning and then teaching what you have learned.

Some people will not like what you have to say. Some people will not agree with what you have to say. But, if you have lived it, if you know your own truth via experience, then other people may disagree with you but you understand that is simply their understanding. Your truth is not their truth.

There is a problem that arises, however. That problem is, people like to form opinions about something that they do not truly understand. Once they have formed that opinion they spread that opinions. But, an opinion is never the truth. How can it be? It is only an opinion. But, how many people realize that? Instead, they believe that what they think is right and therefore they believed what other people think is wrong.

This situation is amplified when people enter into the realms of philosophy. They want to view a deeply personal understanding from the outside. They then want to form opinions about that understanding. But, as they have no basis to understand that philosophy, at best all they can do is speculate. Yet, they present those speculations as facts and this is where many of the problems of life arise.

What you think is not reality. It is simply what you think. If you cannot be honest enough with yourself and with others to admit that fact, then all you have become is a conduit for lies and spreading the falsehoods that have originated in your own mind out to others. Thus, the world becomes engulfed and dominated by the belief of lies.

Have you lived the Zen? If you have not, you cannot understand the Zen. Thus, you should not be speaking about the Zen.

Study the Zen. Learn the Zen. Practice the Zen. Then, and only then, can you speak about the Zen.

The ultimate truth of Zen is that silence is the ultimate form of speech. If you cannot be silent you can never understand the Zen.

* * *
11/Feb/2019 04:09 PM

Just because you don't like what a person has to say does not make them wrong and you right.

When You Realize Someone is Better Than You
11/Feb/2019 09:27 AM

As you pass through life you will undoubtedly periodically come to the conclusion that someone is better than you. This better can come in many shapes and sizes. Maybe a person does something better than you, maybe they are smarter than you in a subject, maybe they are a better athlete than you in a sport, maybe they have a more artistically creative streak than you, and the list goes on. The one defining factor of this realization is that you recognize they are better. Now what?

For some, this realization comes as an earthshaking surprise. How could that person be better than me? For others, this is a constant realization throughout life—an understanding that you know there are those who do things better than you.

What defines a person's life is what they do with this information once it is realized. ...How they react to the other person. ...How they react to the world. And, how they embrace and/or broadcast this realization.

There are some people who live in a constant state of denial about the realities of their life. They see things, they internally understand things, but they refuse to consciously accept those things. For others, they deny all that is obvious. But, the fact of the matter is, this does not change the life reality of the reality; there is someone better than you out there.

With this information and understanding in hand, some people take the high road and acknowledge another person's superiority and try to learn from them. They do this to hopefully become a better example of themselves. Others, however, are lost in their lower self and from this they attack, they judge, they criticize, they attempt to find fault with those who do what they do better than they themselves do it. Where do you find yourself in this equation and are you honest with yourself about how you behave when engulfed in this reality?

The fact of life is, we are all on a pathway of realization. We can either understand this reality, focus on the betterment of ourselves as we try to help with the greater evolution of reality or we can lock ourselves into a mindset of judgment, denial, hurtful behavior, while ultimately damaging not only our own reality and enfoldment but hurting others who encounter our words, deeds, actions, and behavior.

There are people who are better than you. There are people who do things better than you do. Though you may not like this truth, that is the truth. Thus, instead of claiming to be more, know more, and attempt to diminish the greatness of someone else, you should focus on your own evolution; compliment those who do what they do better than you, and perhaps even attempt to learn from them.

Be then better you by realize there are people who are better than you.

Being more is always defined by realizing the better in someone else.

Always Treat People with Respect
08/Feb/2019 07:32 AM

I always treat people with respect. I always refer to other men as, *"Sir."* Whether they are younger than me, older than me, wearing a suit, a uniform, or dirty clothes, I always call them, *"Sir."* This is the same with women. Though I obviously don't refer to them as, *"Sir,"* I always treat them with the utmost respect.

I was having lunch with a friend last week and I said to the waiter, *"Thank you, Sir,"* after he took our order. After the waiter left my friend said that I really shouldn't refer to people as, *"Sir,"* as that puts them on a level above myself. This made me smile. This friend is one of the those people who plays the corporate game in life and is always looking for means to position themselves, so they read the books on the subject to learn how to do just that and so on. But, people deserve respect. Just like all of us, they are trying to survive in a complicated world. It doesn't matter what their job is. It doesn't matter their level of education. They deserve respect.

I think we have all encountered people who speak down to other people. This is particularly the case when a person embodies a mindset of arrogance. They look down on people who may possess a less revered job than themselves, have less money or less education than them, and so on. But, simply because a person believes that they are better or more well positioned than another person does that make it true? No. We are all cogs of the wheel in life. We are all serving a function. You should never treat other people badly or behave in a manner where you project yourself as superior. Because we are all equally important.

If you treat a person with respect perhaps that will elevate their day just a little bit and make them feel just a little bit better about themselves. Negative words, hurtful actions, demeaning behavior helps no one and no thing. Say nice things to people. Do nice things for people. It doesn't matter who they are. It doesn't matter what their job is. It doesn't matter if you know them or not. It doesn't matter if you will never see them again. Treat people with respect. It will make everybody's everything just a little bit better.

* * *
06/Feb/2019 04:42 PM

Most things will be forgotten.

* * *
06/Feb/2019 04:42 PM

The people who are not successful often find a reason to criticize the ones who are.

The Gift of Giving
06/Feb/2019 07:51 AM

Giving is one the highest forms of human interaction that can occur. But, giving is also one of the most misunderstood and misused types of human interaction. Giving is presenting a person with a symbol of our love, admiration, and affection. Giving is also a tool used to manipulate.

For each of us, we have received gifts that truly made us feel happy, good, appreciated, and loved. We have received gifts that truly changed our lives. We have also given gifts as a means of showing our caring—as a way to make a person's life better, more full, and complete. But, what is the sourcepoint of giving and what is the implication?

For me, I have watched in my life as some people have expected gifts. For example, when my one friend's daughter was young, each Christmas they would ask me to buy her the most expensive gift on her Christmas list. That was okay. I didn't mind. But, it did bring the entire question of, *"Why me,"* into the equation.

Also, in a time gone past, back when faxing was the name of the game, my sister-in-law would fax all of her family and friends her birthday or Christmas wish list. I always found that very amusing. I guess you can't receive if you don't ask. ☺

Then, there is the other side of the issue; you give somebody something that you believed was very special and a well thought out gift on your part but they did not appreciate the implications of the gift. I am sure I have told this story somewhere before, but way back in the way back when I gave my very first mala (prayer beads)—a set I had worn and meditated with everyday for a couple of years to a close friend who had enter the spiritual path with me. I truly thought it was a very special and personal gift that he would truly appreciated. He called me later that evening and told me he had given them to some guy he had met and didn't even know. A guy he probably never saw again. Wow! That shook me. Had he given me his first mala I would probably have it to this day. But, to him, he did not put a value on those beads—he didn't put the same value on them as I did. So, he gave them away.

So, what happens when a gift is received in this manner? Does it change the giving? Does it change the intent of the giving? I imagine that something similar to that situation has happened to most of us, on one level or another, as we have passed through life. A gift given but not appreciated. Then what? What did that gift mean?

Sometime, a person takes giving a gift to an extreme level and they put themselves in debt or worse to give that gift. Then what? Then why? Why, if later down the line that relationship disengages?

Then there is the other side of the issue; the not receiving what we believe is needed. I think for most of us there was probably a time in our youth when we asked our parents for something—something that we believed we really needed but they did not give it to us. This may, in fact, be life altering. I known I encountered a situation or two like that in my youth and I have heard similar stories from some of the people that I am close to. ...A gift needed but a gift not received.

Of course, there are those who attempt to buy a person's affection with gifts. Is that bad? I don't know. I guess that depends on a person's inner motivation.

A weird flashback here for you... I was eating in a restaurant in Beverly Hills a number of years ago and Alice Cooper was there with his wife. As a young teenager he was kind of my rock god. I really like what he and his band were doing with music. You know how it is, we all have someone like that in our youth. Anyway, I noticed that when he attempted to pay, his credit card was declined. I guess even the rich and famous have money problems. Anyway, I jumped in and offered to pay. But, he smilingly said, *"No,"* and walked across the street to the ATM to get some money out. This was back in the day when all the ATM cards were not credit cards. There he was, the great Alice Cooper, walking across the street to the bank to get money to pay for his meal. What a sight.

I guess this brings us back to the central focus of this piece, the essence of giving. Giving is a great thing. But, giving is complicated. You know, it seems that there are far more people out there who want to take—take what is not theirs, take from the life of other people, hurt other people, but not give for their taking. They do this with no care for the person they are taking from or for the negative implications of their actions. But, I guess that is a whole other subject...

So, even though giving can be a complicated equation, it is one of the best things that you can do. It is one of the purist forms of good karma that exists. My suggestion, give. Give to those you love. Give to those you care about. Give to those you respect. Give to those you admire. Even give to those you don't like. Because giving always makes everything just a little bit better. It makes it better for those on the receiving end of a gift and it makes things better for those who give the gift. It doesn't have to be big, just a kind word or a kind gesture. Or, it can be big. But, giving (as opposed to taking) always makes life better. Give!

The Energy of Chaos
05/Feb/2019 08:04 AM

Have you ever enter a place or a situation and BAM you were just hit with the energy of chaos? Everything was crazy and there was really no reason for it.

For example, the other day I drove down this one side street and there was one of those big pickup trucks with the big tires jamming out of a parking lot onto the street. He slams on his breaks and begin to makes a three point turn right into the middle of this small, but oftentimes busy, side street. There he is, backing and forthing it, totally holding up traffic. Then, he jams forward but changes his mind and powers back into the parking lot he had just exited from. This time, however, he enters through the small, one-way, exit driveway almost hitting a car that was trying to leave going down the proper pathway. The truck slams on his horn and continue to move forward.

I have no idea what was going through that driver's mind. But, that is often the case when you enter a situation dominated by chaos. It is somebody doing something that is causing a crazy dispersing of energy that is out of control.

Have you ever entered a place; maybe a home or an office or even a car and you could just feel the energy was not right? It was all stirred up, in some crazy manner, for some unknown reason.

Generally, most chaotic or randomly disordered energy situations are instigated by a single person. Think about the times in your life when you have been surrounded by chaotic energy. It was probably brought into play by the actions of one person. The thing is, when an individual emulates a strong energy, that energy takes hold in the environment where they spend a lot of time: be it a car, an apartment, a house, an office, and so on. Thus, if their energy is crazy, when you enter into the abode of their craziness, if you are sensitive to that type of stuff, you will feel it.

If you have encountered and/or interacted with a person who embraces a life dominated by chaos you will understand how that type of energy is not only very disruptive to the on-goings of anything at hand but it very troublesome and even dangerous to the day-to-day evolution of life. I mean, the people who live at this level inhabit a life defined by chaos and thus all that they touch becomes affected by that chaos.

Do the people that live at this level understand what they are creating? Maybe yes, maybe no. For some, they enjoy the control that being the emulator of chaos and craziness gives them over the lives of other people. Though most who live at this level are total out of control of themselves and their mind; they have no self-control. Yet, they either knowingly or not emulate that energy to create a misplaced sense of purpose and power in their life.

So, what happens when you encounter one of these situations? Yes, your life is altered. Though you may not want it to be. But, at least for that moment it becomes dominated by the energy of chaos. What can you do? First of all, stay in control. Don't let that energy overtake you. Don't let it become the dominating factor in your life. Don't let it to cause you to do things that you normally would not do. And mostly, don't fall prey to the false sense of power that it provides that misguided person who is emulating that energy. Don't give them control over your life.

Just as in the martial arts it is taught that deflection is always the best form of self-defense, do that with any chaotic energy situation you encounter. And, we all will encounter them sooner or later... Deflect the energy. And, never let it control you.

The energy of chaos is controllable. But, it cannot be controlled by force. Just like the person who emulates this energy, their life is not defined by the normal standard of a positive existence. Thus, you should not face off with them. Simply allow the energy to pass and then move away from the energy. Because just like in physical combat the person who enters the confrontation expending all of their energy in their assault, they quickly become tired and are then easily defeated. Purify your space with the energy of positivity and control and then you will never fall prey to the chaos instigated by another's person unfettered mind.

Does the Punishment Fit the Crime?
04/Feb/2019 07:37 AM

Have you ever witnessed a person become physically violent because they were mad at another individual? Have you ever witnessed a person yell and scream because they were angry with another individual? Have you ever witnessed a person set about on a course of revenge, attempting to hurt the life of another person, because they were annoyed with another individual? Have you ever behaved in this fashion?

In life, there are always two perspectives: Yin and Yang, if you will. There is the person who does something and there is the person who reacts to that something. There is the person who instigates something and there is the person who response to that something.

Have you ever witnessed a person do something bad to another person and their friends or their family took joy in that person's actions? Have you ever behaved in this fashion?

How a person reacts to what anyone else does is a personal choice based upon a complex set of interpersonal logic and reasonings. But, how many people possess the level of emotional and psychological maturity to consciously chart their reaction to the action of someone else? Most people simply react. They allow whatever emotion they are feeling, based upon whatever inspiration or instigate they feel they have experienced, to guide their actions. Thus, many are driven to do very negative things in life. But, what is the ultimate culmination of any negative action enacted by a specific individual? No matter what the personal justification for that action is, the ultimate result is always negative karma. Yet, no one things about this. When they are yelling, when they are hitting, when they are taking revenge all they are driven by is their own set of negative, uncontrolled emotions.

Is their an answer to this life quandary? The only answer takes place on the personal level. This is the place where a person is in control of themselves to the level where they are not controlled by the actions of others. Is this a hard state of mind to reach? Yes. But, it is an absolutely necessary level of reality to dwell within if you do not want your emotions, generated by the actions of others, to cause you to walk further down the road of creating negative karma, instigated by how you feel about what someone else has done.

* * *

04/Feb/2019 07:15 AM

You can't control what another person does. But, what you say or what you do may influence another person to take action. If this is the case, you become responsible for that other individual's actions.

* * *

02/Feb/2019 10:25 AM

Do you think hurting someone else's life ever makes anything better?

Finding the Truth in the Lies
AKA The Truth as You Know It
02/Feb/2019 08:32 AM

Life provides each person with an interesting pathway to uncover what is factual—what is true. But, how many people consciously follow this path? How many people actually try to uncover the truth? Do you?

The fact is, the major of life's people simply pass though life believing what they are told. This is especially the case if what they are told comes from a source they like, love, or respect. The problem was this method is, however, a lot of falsehoods are propagated without one taking the time to research the source of the information. From this, lies are compounded upon and spread through friends, families, groups, and history.

The other problem in this equation is that many/most people believe what they believe based upon emotion. They feel a certain way about a person, a place, or a thing and from that feeling that believe something. Then, they spread that emotionally based feeling onto someone else who believes them. The problem in all this is, the person is not basing what they are stating on fact, they are simply basing what they believe upon emotion. Their emotion is not necessarily what others should feel but because they are presenting what they are felling to someone else, their words are taken as fact when they are not. They are simply emotion.

When someone tells you something do you immediately believe them? If you do, why do you react in that manner? If you don't, why do you react in that manner?

Each person, as they pass through life, has the ability to uncover the truth. This truth should not be based upon assumption or projection, it should not be based upon emotion or faith, it should be based upon factual research. But, how many people behave in this fashion?

Do you project your feelings to the world and present them as fact? Do people listen to your supposed facts, that are not facts at all? If you behave in this manner you are one of the causes of one of the primary factors that leads to problems with this world. What do you think about that? What facts do you have to support or deny this conclusion?

In life, you can live your life based upon the truth. In life, you can live your life based upon the lies. Who are you? What do you choose to do?

When Things Go Away
01/Feb/2019 07:29 AM

Don't you hate it when things go away. Maybe a restaurant or a café' you like goes out of business. Maybe it's a bar, a nightclub, or even a clothing store. Maybe it is someone you really like moves away or dies. They're gone. They're never coming back. And though you want that something to still be a part of your life, there is nothing you can do to change it. It is no more…

Recently, I just found out that Google+ was shutting down by April. That's crazy; Google is such a massive force in the universe. But, they say the web platform did not have enough interest.

For those of you who do not know, Google+ was a place where you could set up your own website for free. It was a great! An easy to use alternative to having your own website. I set up a few pages there myself (listed below). It was great and everybody could view it. Unlike places like Facebook, where a person has to be on the platform to see the post, Google+ was free to the world. But now, it is going away.

This is all very similar to when who ever it was that had the great idea to change the format and ruined the MySpace platform forever many years ago. They set that change in motion and with that all things internet changed. Though certainly not as social as the old MySpace, Google+ served an important purpose.

Anyway, the pages I have/had on Google+ are listed below. Check them out if you feel like it before they are gone—gone forever…

And, as for life… Things change. Things go away. When they are gone they are gone. As only those of us who appreciated them when they were here can understand, it is a big-big loss when they are no more.

Gate, Gate, Paragate, Parasamgate, Bodhi Svaha.

If you have any thoughts or suggestions, let me know. ☺

* * *

31/Jan/2019 11:38 AM

Will what happens today change your tomorrow?

Will what you do today change your tomorrow?

Will what you do today change someone else's tomorrow?

When you were doing what you were doing today were your thinking about who's tomorrow it would change?

* * *
31/Jan/2019 07:21 AM

Does a baby know what god is?

The Motivation for Your Motivation
29/Jan/2019 08:45 AM

In life, everybody does something. In life, everybody has a reason for doing the something that they do. Some people do what they do with a very conscious intent. They want to achieve an end result. Other people just do to do—they get an idea and they do it. In either case, all of this doing is based upon one person deciding that what they do is something that they want to do. What this life-ideology is rarely based upon, however, is thinking about anyone but the Self.

Think about your life. Think about the things you have done. Think about how the things you have done have affected your life. Think about how the things you have done have affected the life of other people.

Do you ever consciously focus on what you are about to do? Do you ever contemplate how what you will do will affect your life? Do you ever contemplate how what you do will affect the life of another person?

For most, when they actually start to question their motivations they will quickly realize that what they are choosing to do is highly self-motivated. They are doing what they are doing for themselves or for someone they care about. They rarely even consider what effect what they are doing will have on someone else. If they are taking this into considering they are mostly thinking about how they either get what they want from some other person or how they can hurt some person that they may not like. Thus, and obliviously, most everything a person does is based upon a self-motivated mindset.

Whereas much of a person's life is commonly based upon doing only with the perspective of Self in mind, there are also those people who base their life simply upon a reactive consciousness. This situation occurred, that person did that something, or they are simply not in a good mood, thus they become anything but kind and caring. They just reactively react.

If we consciously contemplate this mindset we can easily understand that this is the lowest level of human consciousness. But, think about it, how many people base their entire life simply on reactive consciousness? Think about how many lives have been damaged due to this reactive consciousness. How about your life? How about they lives of those you have encountered and reacted towards?

One can rightly say that a person should not base their life on a selfishness of mind and/or reactive life interactions. One can rightly say that a person should raise their thinking mind to the level where damage is not instigated by embracing their reactive, uncontrolled mind. But, how many people are willing to apply this understanding to their life? Are you?

There is one thing that is very certain in life and that one things is, all one has to do is to look at their own life and their own life interaction to confirm this fact. If you live a life based upon unconscious, uncaring behavior; if you live a life based upon reactive consciousness, not only will you damage the life of other people but, though you may gain moments pleasure from what you have done, your life will also be damaged due to the negative life interactions you have instigated.

So, where does this leave us? Some people have retreated from the world simply to avoid this style of life behavior and/or life interaction. But, most of us cannot or do not want to live a life absent from others. Thus, we must learn a way of coping.

To begin to live a better life, you must take control over your mind. You must chart what you mind is doing, how your mind is motivating you to take certain actions, and contemplate what those action unleash not only in your own life but also onto the world as a whole. The fact is, if you cannot care about others, if you cannot care about what you are unleashing to the world, if you cannot stop your negative, hurtful behavior, you must understand that there will be life consequences. Not only instigated from others around you but simply encountered on the path you have laid out before yourself.

Thus, take the time to know yourself. Care enough to learn how to control yourself. Think about the implications of your actions before you act. And know that all life is based upon how a person lives their life. What you do and why you do it will set the standard for what you encounter next in your life. Care enough to care.

* * *
27/Jan/2019 08:24 AM

As you pass through life you feel what you feel.

Do you ever analyze why you are feeling what you are feeling as you are feeling it?

Do you ever question how what you are feeling is affecting others?

Do you ever question how others feel about what you are feeling?

Buy a Camera and Make Your Own Movie
24/Jan/2019 08:08 AM

Recently, a guy contacted me and wanted to fly me into his city to make a Zen Film. He explained that he really needed my sensibilities in a movie he hoped to create. Initially, I thought that might be fun. Working with an entirely new and unknown group of people who were into *Zen Filmmaking*. But, then I started to see the flaws in this guy's hopes and ideology. Though *Zen Filmmaking* is entirely about freedom—about simply getting out there and doing it, I was being asked to come to a city I had never been to and basically do everything. I mean everything. I decided to pass on the offer and I suggested to the guy, *"Why don't you buy a camera and make your own movie."*

In today's world, you can literarily make a movie with your phone. I have. Or, you can use any number of relatively inexpensive cameras that are on the market. The fact is, it is very doable if you have the focus and the dedication. But, I believe that is the issue, the focus and the dedication. There are a lot of people who want to DO but very few people who will DO.

Sure, I have my advice for budding filmmaking. …Like don't try to mimic what has already been done. Make your own movie, using your own cinematic philosophy, and so on. But, it can be done. And, it can be done relatively cheaply. Not like in times gone past.

This all kind of struck me as interesting when I gave that guy the advice, *"Why don't you buy a camera and make your own movie."* That was something I had said to someone else, way back in the way back when, under entirely different circumstances.

The story, I was making a movie and this guy/my friend (I surmised) was helping me out. He was an actor. I had met him working on the set of someone else's film. And, like so many others, he wanted to break into the Hollywood game. Me, being me, I was charting my own course to achieve that goal. In any case, we were filming one day and I was realizing that we were running late and we were having some technical issues and we should not film this girl he was crushing on very hard that day. He completely freaked out and started yelling and screaming. This obviously really messed with my small cast and crew. It wasn't that I was not going to use the girl. It was just that I realized her scenes would be better filmed at a better location I had in mind and on a different day. In any case, we finished the day. Once home, I left him the message, *"Why don't you buy a camera and make your own movie."*

Though he apologized, we finished the movie, and remained in contact over the next several years; I knew I could never trust him again. That style of reactive behavior is just not healthy for the emulation of art: cinematic or otherwise.

Certainly, on sets, I have seen this style of behavior before and after that occurrence. But, it is just not good. It poisons the fruit. I mean, in worse case, if you are not liking what is going on, leave. I know I have done that. I have done that even in the case of one big A-film I was cast in and on a TV series. …That one was an interesting one… I was cast to do a role in the last (short-lived) sitcom that the great actor James Garner was doing. In any case, we were on the set, we had done the rehearsals, and then Garner shows up. We started to do rehearsals with him and what an asshole! I mean this guy was a total jerk! That was sad because I had always really liked him as an actor. We shot the scene as Garner continued to go off at me and everyone else. They called lunch. I left and never came back. The production company claimed I ruin the story by leaving. My agent got really pissed and dumped me. But me, good or bad, I stood my ground. I didn't throw a fit. I just left. ...And, you wonder what happened to my career in the A-Market. There's your answer. ☺

Anyway... That's just kind of a side note to the story and the point of all this. If you want to make a movie, why don't you buy a camera and make your own movie. Use your phone. Use whatever it is you have. Get out there and film something everyday. It doesn't have to have story structure. Lord knows, my films don't. All it has to have is you doing something. Film it, take it off of your phone or your camera, edit it if you want, and make something! Make art!

This is the same with any art you desire to create. Do it! Draw, paint, write.

Art is based in one person doing one thing. Again, do it! Because if you don't, all your life will be left with is all of those artistic projects you envisioned in your mind but never created.

Don't Blame the Victim for the Crime
23/Jan/2019 03:10 PM

I was walking back to my car after having breakfast at one of my favorite haunts, *The Original Farmer's Market*. As I was walking through the parking lot this SUV started to back up. They didn't notice I was behind them so I just quickly stepped out of the way. No big deal. That kind of stuff happens all of the time. What happened next is what this tale is all about…

Anyway, a middle-aged blonde white woman rolls down her window and angrily yells at me, *"Get out of the way when someone is backing up!"* Wow… Okay… My response, *"This is California and pedestrians have the right of way."*

In that weird sort of way, all this was kind of funny. This was one of those situations that would have been totally forgotten two seconds later but this woman, obviously raging with some misplaced anger, took it to another level. At most, when something like that happens, as a driver, you give the walking person a wave of, *"Sorry,"* and that is that. Not her. I mean, we all make mistakes, every now and then, when we drive. Moreover, she was just such an average looking middle-aged woman yelling at me for a mistake that she made. Very strange…

In any case, she continues, *"Yeah, this is California but you need to watch out."* My thought, *"Isn't it the driver who should watch out?"* I mean, this was not my fault.

I could totally tell this was one of those situation that if this woman had been a man she would have gotten out of the car and tried to start a physical fight. A fight over a very minor mistake that she made.

She concludes, *"You're a fucking asshole!"* My response, *"I'm an asshole and you almost hit me?" "Fuck you,"* she yells. She then flips me off and drives away. Wow, what a situation—what a needless situation.

I think anger is an interesting emotion. I speak about it every now and then in this blog. I speak about it because we all feel this emotion from time to time. I also speak about how some of the people I have encountered in life are controlled by that emotion and from that they hurt or destroy the life of other people and/or their own. Why do some people allow this emotion to take control over their life?

Also, as I speak about periodically in this blog, some people are a selfish, self-motivated creature. They constantly shift internal blame onto someone or something else even when it is their fault. Again, why do they do that?

I suppose those two questions can have many answered all based upon the psychology of the individual. Certain, not having a clearly defined understanding or definition of Self is one of the primary factors that causes anger to rage, uncontrolled, within the individual. Just as misplaced entitlement causes some people to behave badly and uncaringly towards others.

The thing about life is, you cannot control the emotions or the actions of others. Yet, in some cases, like the above described situation, you are forced to deal with the repercussions of the behavior of these other people. This is just the fact of life. And, I believe, in some ways that is sad because so much negativity can be brought to your doorway due to the uncontrolled actions of someone else. I imagine that many of us have had to encounter the anger and to deal with situations created by the anger of someone else in our life. This, when we wanted nothing to do with it.

The answer? There is none. Again, we can't control what other people do. All we can do is be the best, most enlightened, most focused, and in control individual that we can be. This is why we must study emotions like anger. ...Study this emotion in other people and in our self. This is why we must study selfish, self-motivate behavior. ...Study this emotion in other people and in our self. Because if we don't, if we simply react our way through life, what are we? Then, we are nothing more than a middle-aged white woman raging in a parking lot, making all things for all people worse. Then, we are nothing more than the instigator of the crime. An instigator who blames others for our misdeeds.

Be more. Study yourself. Control yourself. Care about others.

Looking for Women in Hong Kong
AKA The Lie is the Limit
22/Jan/2019 07:23 AM

I was walking down the street in Wan Chai the other day and a strange realization came over me. I saw a couple of different Western guys walking by solo. You could see that they were both new to Hong Kong and their eyes were wide open. Wide open and looking in the direction of women. Funny, I thought, that was me forty years ago. But, the fact is, Hong Kong is not an easy place to meet and sex-up and/or fall in love with local women. Go to Bangkok if you want that. But, that's an entirely different story. And, not the point of this piece at all.

People, (men in this case), who can't find what they are looking for in their own (home) environment commonly seek outwards to find a way to fill that need. That need of companionship. For those who possess the bankroll they may travel to distant shores holding onto the belief that there they may have more luck. But, why is that? Well, I think, at least one of the reasons is that once you are on some distant shore you can become anybody. You can tell people anything. If you are staying at a nice hotel, you are set. The game is on. The con is on. You can be anyone or anybody you want to be. Sure, now with the internet it is a little bit easier to check out a person's story. But, for some guy looking for some girl, the sky is the limit—the lie is the limit.

Certainly, these same kind of mind games go on all over the place, used by every local guy seeking every local woman. But, it is so much easier to see the lies when you are of the same culture. Lord knows, back in the day, I believed a lot of things that a lot of women told me out there in the distant reaches of Asia. Stories that turned out to be anything but true.

And, that's the point; all this mind fuck goes both ways. And, the fact is, if a girl is willing to immediately hook up with a guy from a far off shore that is probably going to be gone in a few days, they are probably not the kind of girl you are going to want to bring home to meet mom anyway.

So, what does this tell us about life? People want love. People want to be loved. People want their needs of companionship met. People want their fantasies of lust fulfilled. If these needs are not being fulfilled in a person's own back yard then they may choose to move outwards beyond the realms of the expected in hopes of meeting that fulfiller of illusion. But, illusion is all it is. That dream of having that something that is unknown, that fills that need buried deep within all of us. But, if all you can do is look outside with a dream of fulfillment in your pocket, then how can you ever be fulfilled?

What has to be accepted is that if you are not fulfilled or fulfillable in your own space of life and culture you are not going to find that fulfillment anywhere else. If you can't find that love, that sex, that whatever in your own backyard you aren't going to be able to find out it out there on the hard road. Sure, there are a lot of women (in the case of men) willing to play along. ...Like I used to say regarding my relationship situations in Asia, *"They have a Green Card in one eye and a Dollar Sign in the other."* But, that's all just mind stuff that adds to the chaos of life. And, it's the kind of mind and life stuff that may end up destroying your life.

So, the moral of the story… Sure, go to Hong Kong or Asia if you want. I do it whenever I can. I love it there. But, go there for the right reason(s). Go there for the experience of experience. But, don't go there expecting that you are going to find that missing element of your life: be it love, lust, enlightenment, or whatever. Because if all you do is look outside of yourself for fulfillment, you will never be fulfilled.

Lost and Found
21/Jan/2019 09:31 AM

Have you ever had somebody you hadn't seen in a long time show up unexpectedly at your door? Though it may be good or it may be bad to see them, their arrival was totally unexpected. Why did they come over? Why did they decide to show up? Generally, this situation is based upon someone not having anywhere better to be and them needing a friend or a something... ...Not bad, not good, just reality.

I think back to a person who showed up at my door, back in the days when I was still in high school. He was a year or so older than me and had graduated the year before. Though we occasionally spoke at school, I would not say that we were close high school friends. We did, however, share a mutual interest in Eastern Metaphysics.

I was surprised to see him when he arrived. It was in the evening on a weeknight and I was kind of amazed that he even knew where I lived. He had never been to my apartment before. But, the knock came. I answered the door. *"Hey, what's going on?"* And, from that point we became fast friends for the next few years exploring all kinds of the Eastern teachings that were available at the time and all of the blooming music of the day. Had he never showed up, I imagine that both of our lives would have evolved quite differently.

During this same period, I was over at my girlfriend's apartment one Saturday evening. We were doing all the stuff that teenage love promises. A late night knock came at her door. It was a guy she knew but she wouldn't answer the door. *"I want to make love to you,"* he exclaimed through the locked door. Me, being me, I wanted to go and kick his ass. But, as her mother wasn't home and her not wanting to be responsible for a fight in her building, she held me back and we just waited until he went away. I never really trusted her again after that. For obvious reasons…

In this current world, a lot of stalking takes place. Sadly, I have encountered a few of those situations. Mostly, it has just been people seeking friendship, a part in a movie, or wanting to find out what Scott Shaw is actually all about. A couple of the other times, however, it has been by people who had less than positive intentions in mind.

Again, this brings us back to the question of why people reach out in this peculiar, unexpected manner. Why are they doing it? The answer, they are doing it because they have nothing better to do—nowhere better to be. And, because they are lost in the complexities of Self, and in need of an outlet—an outlet of human interaction. Thus, they concoct a method to make human interaction, with a particular person, possible.

Most people operate from a positive life perspective. They are really not about hurting anyone else. That's good! That's a good thing! But, as we have all heard about, via the news and other media, this is not always the case. Moreover, people are based in desire. They want something from someone else, which is why they contact, stalk, or speak about them in the first place.

No one wants to be alone. Thus, people find methods to not be alone. If you don't have a well-substantiated group of established or ever-growing friends, then you must turn to other methods to reestablish relations and/or meet people. Thus, the knock on the door.

So, what can we learn from all of this? What should you do if someone knocks on your door out of the blue? And, should you go and knock on the door of someone else—someone you knew from times gone past? There is no absolute answer but the question to look to is, *"What is the motivation?" "What is the reason why?"*

Motivation and reason are the bases of who a person is and what a person does. Thus, not only must you always study, define and refine your own reasons and motivations but you must also do the same with other people in your life.

Know yourself. Know your motivation(s) for why you do what you do. Know why you do what you do. And, be strong enough to control what you do if what you do may hurt someone or will not be a positive contribution to the life of any other person you choose to involve in your melodrama. Moreover, study the people you associate with. Study the people who enter your life. Are their intentions pure, good, and beneficial to the greater all? If they are, great! If not, don't answer the door.

* * *

21/Jan/2019 08:47 AM

There are no secrets. There is only what someone does or does not know.

* * *
21/Jan/2019 08:46 AM

When you are speaking about someone else it is easy to make them seem bad or good.

When you are speaking about yourself do you put that same analysis into your description?

* * *
21/Jan/2019 08:21 AM

You can only be lost in fantasy until reality takes hold.

* * *
21/Jan/2019 08:20 AM

If you can get though being tired you usually wake up.

If you can get through being awake you usually get tired.

Why You Do What You Do and What It Does To the World
17/Jan/2019 01:45 PM

I was sitting around waiting for my plane at the Hong Kong Airlines VIP Lounge the other day and I realized I hadn't checked my Facebook page for a few days. So, I went over to one of their computers and was getting ready to sign in. When I got to Facebook I realized that some young guy had left his Facebook account opened and he was already signed in. One of those funny thoughts came to my mind regarding the fact that I could have totally messed with the unknowing young man's life and sent all kinds of messages and stuff like that all kinds of direction via his Facebook account. It made me kind of smile. Of course, I didn't do that. I signed out of the guy's account, cleared the computer's history, and resigned in. But, think about how many people would have done just that. …Done that just that because they could.

Do you ever watch your life? Do you ever watch the behavior of other people in your life? Do you ever allow yourself to walk down the dark road and do things that you, (at least), should know are wrong? But, do you do them anyway? Do you allow people you know to say or do bad or negative things to other people?

Why do you do bad things? Why do you do hurtful things? Why do you do judgmental things? Why do you take what isn't yours? Why do you invade the life of other people?

Do you ever question the things that you do? Or, do you just do because you can do or because you feel like it?

A person's life is forever based on the actions of other people. In many cases, you cannot control those actions. Maybe you make a mistake. Maybe you leave your Facebook account open. Maybe you accidentally allow someone into your life. But, what becomes of your life is always based upon what another person does to your life.

A good person does good things. They do not hurt other people. What does that say about everyone else? What does that say about you?

What do you do with your life and why do you do it? Do you do it just because you can? Do you do it just because no one is looking or you can get away with it? Do you do it hidden behind some sort of mask?

Good is always good. Bad is always bad. Helpful is always helpful just as hurtful is always hurtful.

Just because you can do something does not mean that you should do something.

Make the world a better place. Only do good things.

The Good That You Do and Who You Do the Do To
17/Jan/2019 01:01 PM

I recently wrote a blog about the *Teacher's Pet Scenario* and how this one person, in my distant frame of knowledge, was fired because, as a boss, he provided a negative yearly review about a person who was loved by one of the major mucky mucks of the company. This, right before Christmas. That was uncool, I thought. But anyway… Read the blog if you wish.

All this struck me as interesting as it provides a very clear overview into the reality of life and how some people move up/move forward even when they do not necessarily deserve it. It is kind of like the old Hollywood industry saying, *"It's who you know or who you blow."*

As this situation has unfolded, it has continued to interest me. The aforementioned Teacher's Pet was recently promoted to the position her boss was fired from. This, after a much more qualified and extremely more experienced candidate was passed over for the positive. Why? The *Teacher's Pet Scenario.*

I think if we look to life, especially for those who live in the world of interpersonal interactions, a lot of this style of behavior can be witnessed. There is the term, *"The Peter Principal."* Which, as described by Laurence J. Peter, in the corporate world, people rise to their, *"Level of incompetence."*

Is this why companies fail? Yes. Is this why there is so much disharmony and distrust with companies? Yes. Is this why there is so much hatred for authority within companies? Yes. In fact, this ideology spreads from the corporate world throughout society. People do what they must to be loved, liked, appreciated, or feared. They do this, in many cases, without ever possessing the skillset to truly accomplish what they eventually achieve. Yet, someone within a position of authority likes that person, for whatever reason, and they empowered them even though there are others with a far better skillset that would actually help the company and/or the world in a much better way. Yet, they are not given the chance.

So, what does this tell us about achievement in the Real World? It's the *Teacher's Pet Scenario.* It's the *Who You Know or Who You Blow Situation.* The person who holds the cards forever dominates what you are ultimately allowed to become. Though the person who is handed the undeserved promotion relishes in their accomplishment and power it is that same ego-driven perspective which will ultimate lead to their demise; not only in the job they poorly do but also in life in general because that is just the way it is. Power leads to ego. Power leads to corruption. Power leads to decisions based upon uninformed, personally driven, motivations. When this is the case, then all involved are doomed for failure and life demise.

Have you ever met a person who was handed a position of power? Have you ever met a person who was handed a position of power when there were others more qualified? How did they behave? Look to their life reactions. How did they treat the people who gave them the position? How did they treat the people they now oversee? How did they deal with the fact that they did not possess the skillset to actualize the job they were given? Look to the answers to these question to better understand all life and your personal life. From this, you too may learn that power and position is the ultimate form of failure.

* * *
17/Jan/2019 09:51 AM

Today or tomorrow, does it really matter?

* * *

17/Jan/2019 09:50 AM

It's not about how well people treat you; it's about how well you treat other people.

* * *

17/Jan/2019 09:49 AM

Why does a good person do a bad thing?

Why does a bad person do a bad thing?

Is a good person who does a bad thing actually a good person?

* * *

06/Jan/2019 07:30 AM

Just because a person is nice to you does not mean that they are nice to everyone else. Your assessment of a person should not just be based upon how they treat you but by how they treat everybody.

All Beings Are Bound by Karma
05/Jan/2019 08:37 AM

One of the primary Buddhist concepts, and the first of the *Four Nobel Truths* is the understanding that, all beings are bound by Karma. Though the word, *"Karma,"* is constantly thrown around in modern society, few people actually comprehend this understanding. Here's a little background for you...

The Sanskrit word, *"Karma,"* literally translated, means *"Action."* This word represents the law of cause and effect, *"As you sew, so shall you reap."*

Karma

Karma is one of the most complicated and profoundly philosophical issues each person must deal with in understanding Zen Buddhism and, in fact, life. This is because of the fact, right and wrong, good or bad, are not universally defined in this physical world. Not only does each culture possesses a somewhat differing view of right and wrong but each person holds their own values and individual perceptions of good and bad. Certainly, there are distinct wrongs: hurting someone unnecessarily, forcefully taking something from another person, behaving selfishly, and so on. But beyond these obvious instances, the precise definition becomes lost. For example, what about when you hurt someone unintentionally? Or, while pursuing the spiritual path you must leave someone behind, thus, causing him or her to suffer at your absence?

The question of Karma is amplified when people justify the wrongs they are performing for what they believe to be a just cause. For example, how many people have died in wars on this Earth motivated by religious idealism?

Perhaps even more disconcerting is the case of individuals who continually cause physical and emotional pain to other people. Yet, somehow their life seems to continue forward in an unhindered path of success and acquisition. When justifying their negative Karmic actions these people oftentimes allude to the fact that they had a bad childhood, are getting back at the world for what was done to them, or due to negative peer influence they were guided down the wrong road. Though these may be psychologically valid rationalizations, none-the-less, negative actions have taken place, often times injuring good people.

On the other side of the issue, there are those individuals who continually provide a positive service to the world. Yet, they are confounded by continued negative encounters. Why should adverse experiences happen to these people if they are expounding good to humanity?

The philosophic debate on the nuances of Karma has gone on for centuries. And, it will continue. In ancient Vedic scriptures, three levels of Karma are defined which may provide some insight into the various types of Karmic actions.

The three levels of Karma are:

1. Sanchita Karma, *"Accumulated Karma."*
2. Prarabdha Karma, *"Actions which create Karma."*
3. Kriyamana Karma, *"Current actions."*

Sanchita Karma

Sanchita or *"Accumulated Karma"* is the Karma that you have previously substantiated. *Sanchita Karma,* not only defines actions that you have taken in this life, but also actions that you performed in previous incarnations. Many believe that this is one of the primary components that go into the formation of an individual's personality—as they are acting out a life style and mindset that they substantiated in a previous life.

The understanding of *Sanchita Karma* is also used to define why seemingly good people encounter negative events in their life. It is understood that though they may now be very good, in a previous existence they must have created adverse Karma. Thus, they suffer in this lifetime.

Certainly, in the Western world, the concept of paying for sins from a previous life strikes an adverse chord in many people. This is because of the fact that they believe that their current body is their only body and even if they do accept the theory of reincarnation, why should they have to pay the price for an existence that they no longer have any control over? This is where the belief systems indoctrinated by religion comes into play in the definition of Karma. For example, a Buddhist would simply let go of philosophic questioning and relinquish him or herself to accepting the understanding of *Sanchita Karma* as fact. Thus, any life occurrence, be it positive or negative, is quickly rationalized and accepted as Karma.

Prarabdha Karma

Prarabdha Karma is the Karma that has come into existence due to past actions. Illustrative of this type of Karma is the individual who performs negative acts, for what ever physical, emotional, or psychological rational, and then later in their life they encounter unfavorable situations. These events may take place in the next life, the distant future, or may happen almost instantaneously. This understanding provides some solace to people who have been wronged by others, as they know, sooner or later, that unjust individuals will have to pay the price for their actions.

It is additionally understood, at this level of Karmic understanding, if one's Karmic debt is paid up, then any Karmic retribution for a negative act will be incurred relatively quickly, as there is not a long backlog of wrongs waiting to be repaid.

Prarabdha Karma not only details the events that occur as a result of adverse Karma but it is also equally applicable to positive Karma, as well. This can explain why the rare case of a truly negative person, in this life, continually encounters seemingly positive experiences; they were a very good person in a past life.

Kriyamana Karma

Kriyamana Karma is the actions you take that lay the foundations for either positive or negative Karma in the future.

Some people were born into economically poor living conditions, dysfunctional families, or have had a childhood corrupted by bad influences and occurrences. Others have experienced a relatively positive childhood only to be impacted by negative situations, as they have grown older. For decades, Sociologists and Psychologists have attempted to draw conclusions to why an individual follows a particular path in life based in their foundational attributes. Though there is, no doubt, quantitative validity to some of their findings, it must be ultimately understood that we each are the masters of our own destiny. At any point in life, be it before you instigate any adverse Karma or post having unleashed a plethora of negativity, you can take back your life and choose to consciously move forward—doing good things for the world, creating good Karma, even while you suffer the inevitable repercussions for actions you have taken in the past.

Certainly, most of us have encountered influences in our lives that were not of the purest content. Additionally, due to innumerable psychological factors we have all walked down impure paths with people we should not have. Under these influences most of us have all performed acts that we now can see as, *"Bad Karma."* Knowing this, you have two options in your life. One, you can hold on to those experiences and allow them to set a pattern for the rest of your life. Two, you can consciously let go of the past and move forward into a world where you will never allow negative people or situations to guide you again. With this more positive approach, you allow yourself to live each new moment of life in a positive fashion; following the path to self-realization while you do good things for all those you encounter.

Creators of Karma

From ancient Vedic scriptures we learn that once one's personality is initially set in motion by *Sanchita Karma,* the individual then moves forward into life choosing to act out one of three types of Karma: *Sattva, Rajas,* or *Tamasa.* These three types of Karma parallel the understanding, known in

Sanskrit as *Gunas,* or *"The Three States of Consciousness."*

Sattva is the pure state. *Rajas,* is the active, passionate state. *Tamas* is the dark, overripe state.

The Sanskrit word, *"Karman."* is used to describe an individual who is creating a specific type of Karma. Thus, an individual is a *Sattva Karman, Rajas Karman,* or a *Tamas Karman.*

The *Sattva Karman's* actions are pure, precise, and directed towards a higher good, each step of their life. A *Rajas Karman's* actions are all performed from a sense of ego—everything is done for the betterment of him or herself. A *Tamas Karman's actions* are performed from a dark, deluded, and confused state of mind—serving no one and no thing.

Karma and the Human Being

Existing in a human body means that everyone, no matter how holy, is bound by Karma. It must be ultimately understood that no act is wholly good and bad. What may benefit one may cause pain to another. Thus, as we are bound by the complexities of human existence and good and bad will remain an individual's perception.

The Zen Buddhist does all that he or she can do to create a positive world: forgiving those who have hurt him or her, helping those who need help, guiding those who need guidance. Any action is attempted from only the most pure of motivations. Understanding that, ultimately, each person is their own person, with their own emotions, desires—cultural and psychological influences.

You cannot make everyone happy. Thus, the Zen Buddhist walks their path, embracing life and attempting to do the most possible good each step of the way.

* * *
04/Jan/2019 12:14 PM

Any answer to the question, *"Why,"* is at best a personal excuse.

* * *

04/Jan/2019 12:11 PM

Right now, who are you hurting and why?

Right now, who are you helping and why?

I Hope I Get to Heaven
Before the Devil Knows I'm Dead
04/Jan/2019 09:18 AM

As someone who has spent their entire life trying to make things a little bit better via teaching, helping, and creating, I am always surprised and/or shocked by the people who attempt to throw roadblocks in that pathway. I am forever sent to wondering what is their motivation.

In life, we have this very short time period to get anything done. In youth, yes, you look to the future and it seems like a pathway of forever. But, the closer you get (and you get closer every day) to that final curtain; you realize that it was not much time at all.

In that time, all you can do is what you can do. It is what you do, in that time, that either makes a positive difference or it does not.

Have you ever had a cup or a glass or a breakable object that you really liked? Then, one day, you dropped it and it was broken. Or maybe, someone else knocked it over and they broke it for you. You quickly realize, things in life are very easy to break but they are virtually impossible to repair. Yet, how many people are out there, spending their life-time breaking their own things and/or breaking the things of other people? How about you?

As I have passed through life I have observed that most people do not take notice of their life; they simply live it until it is gone. As I have passed through life I have watched as many people have wanted something, went after it, but when they got it, it did not fulfill the projected desire that they hoped it would satisfy. Thus, they were left wanting something else and willing to do whatever it takes to fill that void in their existence and this equaled their walking over others and damaging this life-place to gain whatever current fantasy they possess. As I have passed through life I have observed as many a person has felt that they have the right to attack, break, hurt, or destroy the things and the life of another person simply because they have found a method to do just that. What is their motivation? Though they will most likely deny it to the end, it is based upon two primary concepts: jealousy and/or ignorance. Jealousy of what another person has gained or obtained and ignorance about understanding the human condition.

As a person who bases their life upon learning, trying, teaching, and creating, I have occasionally found myself at odds against the-powers-that-be and some person or persons that somehow has gained a foothold on dominance of a specific realm of existence. Though I attempt to avoid those people and the situations they create, sometimes I am forced to walk into the lion's den and it doesn't feel good. Why does a person who cares about others, seeks to find the goodness in all people, and tries to help by whatever means possible need to encounter the demons? I don't have an answer to that question but I guess I can surmise, that's just life. There are those people out there who do not base their existence on caring, on giving back, on helping, and on creating. Instead, they base their existence on finding a means of unleashing misguided power and damaging the life of someone else. Sure, they may have a reason. Sure, they may have a motivation. But, all they care about is the power they possess to break that glass, which is easy. They never master the skills to put that glass back together, which is much-much harder and takes much more technique and capability.

So, what does this teach us? What we can learn is, as you pass through life, hopeful you will be one of the good ones. One of those people who only tries to help, to give, to create, to restore, and never hurt. But, be warned, even for you, one of the good ones, be prepared as the devil may come knocking at your door. If he does, hopefully you will be able to keep that door locked or have a way out. Hopefully, you will have a way to get to heaven before the devil knows that you are dead.

Those Who Have Walked the Road Before You
03/Jan/2019 08:17 AM

Life is a pathway of evolution. We are born, we learn, we evolve, and we become. What we become is based upon what we desire to become and the people who influence us in our becoming. Whether we want to admit it or not, people guide us as we pass through our life. Some of these influences are accidental. Some of these influences as sought after. Some of these influences are paid for. Whatever the case, we learned from those who have walked the road before us.

We too are the influencers of others. Others look to us for our understanding and our guidance. Some people relish in this life position. They seek it out. They are the first to provide their thoughts and give their advice to others. There are also those people who do not desire this responsibility. They know that by guiding someone, suggesting or telling them what they should do, they become the responsible party in that person's actions. That person's deeds become their own karma.

No matter what the situation, we each learn from others as well as we guide others. What we learn is what we have to teach but that is a double-edged sword. If we learn good and pure life behaviors and activities, then that is what we impart. If, on the other had, we learn hurtful and devious life behaviors and activities that too is what we impart. Where do you find yourself in this equation?

Life is a process of learning and then teaching others. An ideal life is represented by someone who learns good things, learns from their bad experiences, formulates a positive frame of mind, and then consciously spreads what they have learned to others.

Look at your life. Look at the people you have encountered. Look at the people who have influenced you, both in a positive and a negative manner. Look at the people you have influenced in both a positive and negative manner. What have you learned? Have you been strong and focused enough to realize what is good; good for you and good for others or have you allowed yourself to fall down the well of self-motivated, unthinking, and uncaring activities? And, is that behavior what you have demonstrated to others?

At the root essence of understanding life, it must be realized that we are all interactive beings, we are taught and we are trained by those who have walked the road before us, we are also the trainer of people who look to us and our life experiences and our life behaviors for who and what they should become. What are the examples you draw from? Are they good, wholesome, and pure? What are the examples you provide? Are they good, wholesome, and pure?

We each are responsible for what we take in and what we do with that information. We each are responsible for what we spread out to the world. Who did you follow on the road that you walk? Who is following you? What did you learn and what are they learning? If you do not think about this, if you do not contemplate the impact you have at each stage of your life, all that is created is world of people who do not know any better. All they will learn is taking, hurting, demanding, and unleashing. Is this the right way to live life?

Study the road you walk. Define who you learn from. Define what you teach others. Be a conscious conduit as you walk the road of life.

Burn Your Poetry
02/Jan/2019 12:43 PM

Certain people embrace the arts. Whatever that art form may be; an artist, at their core, has a vision of art. They have an inspiration. They have a reason to create. This becomes the motivation for their life.

Many artists spend their entire life doing nothing but creating art. Whether others ever view their art or not is unimportant. As they are an artist, that is what they must do; create art.

You can never explain the mindset of an artist to a non-artist, as they will never and can never understand. They can like and they can dislike, they can question why the artist creates their art. But, as they do not possess that inner inspiration, they can never know what the artist truly feels.

At the heart of art is the inspiration to create. The artist feels that something and must create that something in whatever medium they visualize that art to take form. But, in the creating, something is also lost.

There is no artist alive who is one-hundred percent satisfied with what they have created. Yes, they may like some of their creations more than others. But, there is always that lacking, that what is missing, that something else it should have been.

Here we find the folly of art. The missing element to the puzzle. Though art is visualized with-in, it is something that must be actualized with-out. Art is formed in the mind but it must take form outside of the mind. Here is where the disconnect occurs.

What is in your mind is always perfect. It is always the way you want it to be. Once something moves from your mind to physical reality, this is where the difference between theory and reality occurs. Thus, art is never perfect. It is never truly what the artist visualized in their mind. And, if it is not a perfect representation of the art formed in the mind, it is never the perfect projection of artist. At best, it can only be a representative image; imagined but never fully realized.

Many artists make art so their art will be viewed. They create art because they feel they have a message/a vision to covey. Whether their art is in the form of drawing, painting, writing, movement, or music, what an artist visualizes inside of their mind, they wish to project to the world.

Here again, we find a flaw in the methodology. As we now understand, the art in the mind of the artist is never the perfect form of what was in their visualized consciousness and thus it is never absolute perfection. At best, it can only be what it is.

Here, in some cases, even the artist loses track of their reason for creating art. For some/many they create art as a means of self-expression, as a means to express their thoughts and the interpretations of life to the masses. But, is that art or is that ego? Is believing that you have something that someone else should view or should hear art or ego? If it is ego, than how is that true art?

Once upon a time, in a time not so long ago, there were a group of people that created art and then discarded their art. They would paint their paintings, show their art to their friends, and then destroy their paintings—they would read their poetry to their friends and then burn their poetry.

These artists lived the perfect essence of art. Create, display, destroy.

Though this was only one philosophy based in the dissemination of art, it is undoubtedly one of the purist. For by following this philosophy, the artist was allowed to create, while embracing the purist form of art and while also removing one of its primary deterrents, the ego of longevity—creating art to make one's self famous and/or known.

Are you an artist? If you are, do you ever ask yourself why do you create art? Do you ever question your motivation for creating art?

If you are an artist and if you are not creating art simply as a necessary element of your life—if you are creating solely as a means to find notoriety, fame, or fortune, than you are missing the entire point of art. If you are an artist, question why are you creating art?

The Path of Least Resistance
30/Dec/2018 07:32 AM

I had this weird flashback the other day. I remembered back to the time when I got my first car when I was sixteen and I would drive it to high school. It was a weird thing. I would turn left out of my apartment building's parking lot, drive down Hobart, the street that I lived on, turn right onto Sunset Blvd., and if I drove at exactly thirty miles an hour the signal lights were timed so that I could get all the way to Hollywood High School on Highland without ever having to stop for a red light. I honestly don't know how or why I figured that out but somehow I did. It was a very Zen experience.

But, then came the girls and the girlfriends and the friends that needed me to pick them up and all that kind of high school stuff. Times and pathways changed and it was no longer so Zen of a driving experience. The path of least resistance was lost.

You know, as we pass through life it seems that this is always the case. We find something, we do something, maybe we acquire something and for that moment of its own perfection we are allowed to live in its perfect essence. Then, comes all of the rest of the life stuff: the people, the places, the interactions, equaling the emotions and the desires. We are removed from the perfection we once knew.

For some, they are allowed to shed all of that life stuff. They are given the means to survive while being allowed to experience nothing but the abstract purity of suchness. But, for all of the rest of us, we have to go to high school, we have to learn our subjects, we have to take our tests, get our jobs, pay our bills, and support those that we love. It is not easy.

The moral of the story… When you find those moments of perfection—when you experience those perfect paths of least resistance, embrace them and love them. Because, in life, if you live life, they are probably going to be few and far between.

Lies Are Small
29/Dec/2018 08:31 AM

Most of us, as we have passed through our lives, have encountered a situation where someone has lied to us. Many of us have lied to other people. In each of these cases the person who is lying believes, at least in their own mind, that they have a reason for telling that lie. As self-serving as that logic may be, that is his or her motivation for telling someone something that is not true.

The majority of lies are what one person says to another person. Yes, one person may be telling the same lie to several people, either individually or in a group setting, but it is one person saying one thing that is not factually based.

Most lies are told to protect a person or to make them appear to be something grander than they actually are. Denying responsibly is also one of the greatest causation factors for lying as is one person wanting something from someone else. Some people are, in fact, simply pathologic liars. They lie about everything. Those people are very hard to be around.

When you are lied to, and if you find out you were lied to, most people become very upset. This is due to the fact that from that lie they created an entire life-scape in their own mind. They may have done things that they would not have done if they had not been lied to, thereby creating an entirely different set of life circumstances than they would have encountered if they had not been lied to.

No matter what the liar's reason is for lying, most lies are very small. They are what one person says to another person. Yes, that lie may cause that other believing person to do things they would not have done if they had not been lied to—yes, it may make the person very angry when they find out they were lied to, but a lie generally only affects one person or a small group of people. Even if a person tells a lie to a family, it is only that family that hears and believes that lie. Think about it, a family is a very small group of people compared against the larger population of the world.

I have the one elderly individually, in my extended family, who for some reason has concocted this lie that he was a member of the CIA. As the years have gone on, this lie has become more and more elaborate. For example, at his eightieth birthday party he went into a whole discourse about all of his covert ops and all of the assignations he was responsible for. One of the other family members noticed my annoyance for being forced to listen to this guy's bullshit and when asked, I answered, *"Have you ever known anyone who worked for the CIA? If you have you would never know it."* And, that's just the thing, a CIA assassin doesn't brag about their deeds.

The fact of the matter is, this man was never even in any branch of the U.S. Armed Forces. This, back in a time when everyone was drafted unless they had a medical or some other type of deferment. In terms of the basis for his lie, this man was a civilian contractor for the Army Corp of Engineers, so he got sent to Asia. Back in the day, they would put advertisements in the back of magazines like Popular Mechanics, *"See the world."* If a person had some skillset, like in the case of this man, clerical training, you could be hired and set overseas for a couple of years. That's what he did. He then came back married and lived a very good life. I don't know why that isn't enough for him? But, it is not. Thus, this ever-growing elaborate lie.

But, here's the thing. Who does this lie affect? No one; not really. Sure, the family hears his stories and most believe him. But, what does that change? It changes nothing. It does not affect the greater scheme of reality on any level and it does not change anyone's life. And, that's the thing about all lies, they are very small. They only affect the people who they are told to and the people who believe them.

We all want to be superheroes. We all want to live a grand life. But, does lying about who we are, change who we are? No. No matter how many lies you tell, at the end of the day, all you are is what you are. All you have done is what you have done. Good or bad, that is reality. You can lie about yourself if you want to. You can exaggerate your achievements if that makes you feel better about yourself. Or, you can just be yourself. That is Zen.

If you lie to someone, you may get what you want. But, you may also hurt that person that you are getting that something from.

All life is based upon what you choose to do with your time here in this life place. If you base your time upon a lie, a lie will be your only legacy. Though only one, two, five, or ten people may know of your lie, that lie was never the truth. So, no matter how small your lie may be, your lie will never be the truth, and any lie you tell will only cement you to a life defined by that lie.

Who do you ultimate want to be? What do you ultimately want your life to be defined by, a lie or the truth?

Nine Months to Live
28/Dec/2018 09:09 AM

I was having breakfast in a restaurant the other day and there was an older gentleman who came in and sat down over at the counter. He began speaking with a lady who was also sitting there. As their conversation evolved, I heard him tell her, *"The doctor gave me nine months to live."* The lady was fairly shocked to hear this, as I believe we all would be. But, he was very calm about it.

Oncoming death is a very strange thing. Most people I have known, who have died, have done so very quickly. A heart attack, motorcycle crash, OD, suicide, or a gun shot. Even the people I have known that have been diagnosed with a life threating illness didn't find out until it was their last days. So, the entire process of dying only lasted for a very short period of time. There was only one person I have known that was warned years in advance and he continued to behave like a total jerk right up until the end. It was only at that point that he was making the phone calls of apology.

But, think about it, it must be a very strange thing to know that death is coming very soon. Certainly, in the case of this man, he must have been experiencing some symptoms, which is what brought him to the doctor in the first place. But, what I have seen for most people in that situation is that the doctors give them false promises. If you have this treatment... If you take this drug... Then, maybe... But, to just be handed the verdict, dead in nine months, that must be very strange.

Health and being healthy is something that most of us take for granted. We don't even think about being unhealthy or being on the road to rapid death until we become sick. But, sick is a horrible place to be. I mean, think about, it feels terrible. The sad thing is, the sicker you are, and the closer you get to death, the more terrible you feel. I always believe that the people who die hard must have a lot of negative karma swirling around them where as the people who are clean go quickly.

But, the fact is, we are all going to die. Forever, there has been a lot of talk of this Whether it has been from the people who think they know about what the Native Americans have believed onto New Age Gurus. But, all of that is just mumbo-jumbo. When you approach that great wall of ultimate change whom are you going to be as you come close to it and whom are you going to be as you pass through it?

Certainly, I say to everybody, try to live a good life. Try to help everybody, even the people you may not like. Try to do good things and say good things. Try to make this life place a better place. Because really, that is all you have, your ability to do good things and removing as many bad elements from life a possible. Because when you walk down that finally pathway towards death, all you will be is what you yourself created. The better you have lived, the better you will die, because at least you can believe that you helped and did not hurt.

What are you doing today to prepare yourself for that final passageway?

* * *
28/Dec/2018 08:43 AM

What do you do when you don't have anything to do?

* * *
27/Dec/2018 12:02 PM

Sometimes you must turn around to see what you have missed.

* * *

27/Dec/2018 12:01 PM

You never see the sun at night but sometimes you can see the moon during the day.

GIGO AKA Bad Thoughts Equals Bad Actions
27/Dec/2018 07:52 AM

When I was in grad school, in the early 1980s, I took a couple of courses on computer programming. I didn't do very well in them but I did come away with an important concept that affects all of life; namely, GIGO: Garbage In, Garbage Out. Meaning, poor input always equals poor output. In many ways, this concept goes hand-in-hand with elements of *The Eightfold Path* of Buddhism.

In basic terms, *The Eightfold Path* teaches that a good life is founded upon doing the right thing. Right Thought, *Samma Sankappa,* leads to Right Action, *Samma Kammanta,* and so forth.

Think about this, why do you think what you think? What are your thoughts based upon? For many, in fact most, their thoughts are programmed into them by the people they associate with and the things they allow to come into their mind.

Certainly, family and friends have guided your life; how you think and what you do. Add to this the books you read, the movies you watch, and the music you listen to and you have become an emulating example of all of those inputs. If those inputs have been very positive in nature, than, more than likely, you emulate those positive transmissions. If, on the other hand, those inputs have been negative, then that is what you most likely output to the world and the people you interact with.

The fact is, many people do not have very much control over what they emulate. They are simply programmed to behave and think in a certain manner and that is how they pass through their life.

Due to the people they associate with, they must maintain a persona—they must act a certain way. Thus, most people rarely evolve as they pass through life; they simply exist with the programming they were provided with. How about you?

It is very easy to trace your life; what you and your life have become and why you have followed that path. Simply look to your past and you can easily remember the events and the people that caused you to do positive things and the events and the people that caused you to do negative things. The problem is, most people do not possess the will of mind to take a look at the causations factors of their life. They do not study their past that lead to who they are today. They simply exist in a state of oblivion doing what they do with little or no thought. From this, there is no personal life evolution and from this negative events, that a person has lived or has witnessed, are reimagined and reenacted.

A person's life programming comes from many sources. Think about the movies you have watched. Without a doubt some of the most memorable scenes are those that invoke an intense emotional response. Certainly, we each understand that is simply an actor portraying an action on screen but these moments of intensity are created to invoke an emotional response in the individual, for that is the known method that makes the audience remember the film, the actors, and the filmmaker. Again, this is a formula used to guide (program) the mind of the viewer. Thus, those who watch a lot of horror films are programmed in a certain manner and are caused to think a prescribed set of thoughts just as those who only watch love stories are programmed in a unique manner.

Though this is a very simple example of how thought leads to action, it is, none-the-less, a very easy one to chart. Think about it. Think about how what you place into your field of experience has programmed your mind.

The thing is, life is based in choice. The problem is, most people do not possess the mental aptitude to actually make conscious choices in their life, guide their own development and destiny, and program their own existence. They simply follow the path that they were programmed to follow. If their life is GI then they emulate GO. How about you? What do you do? Why do you do it? Who guided you to do what you do and encounter life and people in the way that you do? And, can you be strong enough to reprogram you?

Predator
26/Dec/2018 10:04 AM

Since the dawning of the #metoo movement and other recent social uprisings there has been a lot of talk and calling to task of the people who are deemed as predators. This is a good thing, I believe. A lot of people have gotten away with a lot of bad stuff for a very long period of time.

As I have discussed in this blog in the past, this movement has also been used to attack innocent people, however, motivated by whatever personally concocted anger that one person has focused on another specific individual. A person who does that; are they not also a predator?

What is a predator? I believe it is someone who attacks a venerable individual. There are many definitions of venerability, particularly in this digital age, but a predator is someone who seeks out that vulnerability and attacks an oftentimes innocent person via that vulnerability.

Certainly, we see predatory behavior in the news, in movies, and on TV all the time. Doesn't it make you feel really horrible when you watch a women being physically attacked in a scene in a movie? If it doesn't, it should. Or, a man being physically assaulted by a group of men on a TV show. That is horrible predatory behavior. But, that is on the screen. It is not real. Or, is it? Is not showing that element of human behavior simply a projection of what actually takes place in life?

This brings us to the news. Though you normally do not see these acts of predatory violence taking place in news footage, they are spoken of quite often. So yes, they are real.

Have you ever known a predator? Have you ever known someone who attacks someone else? Most people will answer, *"No."* Though this is the standard answer, it is not necessary a true answer. Yes, most people do not know people who go out of their way to beat, rape, or steal from people, but think of the subtle elements of these acts that take place all the time.

Have you ever instigated a fight? Then you are a predator. Have you ever instigated a sexual act that was not completely desired by your partner? Then you are a rapist. Have you ever taking something from someone without his or her consent? Then you are a thief. Of course, the list goes on. But, what this explains is that there are predators everywhere.

Look at the internet. Look at how people steal other people's music, art, ideas, and films all the time. Look at all the bad things people say about other people. Yet, they are free to do this. Are the people who steal on the internet predators? Yes, they are. Are the people who say hurtful, negative, or judgmental things on the internet predators? Yes, they are. Yet, those who do this generally delight in the experience of their power.

This power over others is the source of predatory behavior. It is what gives people that sense of conquering others. Though what they are doing may not be a seemingly violent or vile act, what they are doing is no less predatory. Yet, how many of the people who behave in this fashion feel sorry for their actions? How many of them apologize for their actions? How many of them attempt to repair any damage that they have caused by their actions? Very few. Thus, they are the absolute definition of a predator.

Currently, we are living in a place in history of people calling out predatory behavior. Yet, predatory behavior takes place all around us. Most people watch it in the movies and on TV, most people read or write it on their computer or phone screens. Yet, no one ever calls them out. At best, people take one side or the other and either love or hate the person who is doing whatever it is they are doing. Thus, all of these current movements are doing very little to actually curb predatory behavior. Yet, many people are very willing to call one person a predator when they, themselves, are no less guilty.

Who are you? Do you hurt, injure, steal, lie, cheat, judge, or hurt any other person in any way for any reason? Then you too are a predator. Think about it. Think about it before you do the next thing that you do. Think about what implications your words or your actions will mean to the life of another person.

You Can Say Whatever You Like But Until You've Lived It You Don't Know It
26/Dec/2018 08:11 AM

In life, people have a propensity to always have an opinion and to share that opinion to everyone, anyone who will listen. That's fine. There is nothing wrong with this. Some people, the loud mouths, constantly share their opinion in a much more brazen fashion, however. Some may even argue and fight to have their opinions heard over the masses while others spread their thoughts, beliefs, and attitudes in a much more sublet and devious fashion. But, there is one fact that is easily witnessed in anyone who bases their life upon spreading their opinions. That fact is, they don't really know what they are talking about because they have not lived that of which they speak.

Take a look at yourself. I am sure you have a number of opinions about a number of things. Pull one of those opinions out of your mind and take a long, hard look at it. Why do you have that opinion? Why do you think what you think about that subject? In fact, why are you thinking about that subject at all?

In life, there is life. In life, there is what you do with your life. In life, there is what you have experienced but then there is the everything else. There is the what you want to do, the what you hope to do, the what you have heard others have done, and the what you think about the this or the that but you only have secondhand knowledge on the subject. Yet, you think about it anyway. How many things—how much of your life do you spend thinking and having opinions about something that you have not lived?

What is your vocation? What is it that you actually do to feed yourself and your family and to put a roof over your head? I always believe that is the best place to start whenever you begin an inquiry into your Self and your life actions. Because that is the basis of your life.

For most, their occupation has very little to do with what they have an opinion about, because that is their reality. Yes, they may love or hate their job. Yes, they may love or hate the people they work with but there is little thought put into that process beyond the reality of its own reality. It is the everything else that people think about and want to voice their opinion about.

For example, due to my vocation(s), I am often brought to the subject of filmmaking and art and how people focus much of their life opinions on these subjects. But, virtually none of the people who express their opinions on these subjects have any basis for their knowledge. Yes, they may like what they like and dislike what they dislike but they have never entered the process. Thus, and for example, they have no idea of what it takes for an actor to actually land a role in a film and all of the levels of rejection they must face to reach that pinnacle. Because, and I can say this from experience, if you have never gone through the process of fully immersing yourself and entering the film game; seeking and finding an agent, going to audition after audition, getting rejected, until you finally land a role and get a featured or a speaking part, you have no idea of the mental fortitude it takes to achieve that end goal, knowing that the majority of people who try, never get anywhere in their quest. Even if a person gets to say one line on screen in a major film or television show they have achieved a great thing.

Something that most, even those who attempt to gain that crown, will never actualize. Yet, people who have never even tried to walk that path talk and criticize. They speak about something they have no idea about.

Not to belabor on this subject but actual filmmaking is an equally great challenge. Sure, it has become much easier as the digital age has come upon us, but to actually possess the mental focus to create a story, form a cast and crew, get that story on film, edited it, soundtrack it, find a distributor, and release it; that takes an intense amount of mental focus. Yet, that is one of the main sources of people's opinions, a film that they have watched. But, they have no inner knowledge about what went into its creation. Therefore, what does their opinion actually mean?

I have just used the film industry as a simple example. But, think about how many people discuss this subject. Think about how many people have an opinion about a performance or a film. Now question, how many of those people who possess those opinions have actually ever truly entered the game and lived the process. This, therefore, become the perfect example of how people waste their life basing their existence upon creating opinions and listening to the opinions of others.

Opinions are not based in fact or true knowledge.

I have used an art form to establish this point. But, think about all of the people who have opinions about the life of other people. How many times have you heard a person discussing the life or the life choices of someone else? How many times have you, personally, instigated a discussion like that? But, what do you truly know about that person and what do you know about what has caused them to live the life they have lived and make the decisions they have made? Yet, you and others talk.

All life is based in the reality of one person. The one person who is living that life. Yes many, in fact most, turn the focus away from the development of their own inner self leading to a better person creating a better human condition for all. But, that is the folly of human existence. That is *Maya*. People look away from themselves so they do not have to look internally. So they do not have to focus on themselves and embrace and perhaps rectify their own inner flaws.

Here's the assignment: Next time you find yourself voicing an opinion—an opinion that you have no true life knowledge to base that opinion upon; stop yourself. Question, *"What is the basis of my knowledge?"* Question, *"What is my basis of knowledge for the person or the subject I speak?"* Then, focus on yourself and question, *"Why do I even care about what I am speaking?"*

Next time you encounter someone else voicing an opinion—an opinion that they have no True Life knowledge to base that opinion upon; stop them and question, *"What is the basis of your knowledge. What is the basis of the knowledge of the person or the subject you speak?"* Then, ask them, *"Why do you even care about who or what you are speaking about?"*

Know yourself. Know why you do what you do. Know why you have lived what you have lived. Use that knowledge to help others. That is the only opinion worth possessing—the only opinion worth presenting to the world.

**Saying What You Mean,
Meaning What You Say**
25/Dec/2018 11:27 AM

I was a recently at a wedding and when the bride got up to give her post-ceremony speech she made the statement, *"I found the perfect man. All of those men who came before were just dessert."* Okay… That's a bit strange. I mean, how would you feel if the woman you just married referenced the men who came before you as dessert? Isn't dessert a good thing?

To tell the backstory about this woman, she's very nice. I've known her for the better part of thirty years. And yes, she did get around (a lot). Sure, I am sure she was always looking for that perfect guy and it just didn't happen until now. But, dessert?

This all goes to the point and the parcel of what people say, how they say it, and what they mean by what they say. I am sure she meant what she was saying as a compliment and she didn't really mean to diminish her new hubby. But, it just came out weird.

A similar situation was brought up to me a few weeks ago. I was hanging out with some extended family members, and out of nowhere, one of the wives of the equation brought up the fact that the guy who gave the speech at her wedding discussed the groom's previous wife. Wrong! Even then I could not believe he was saying that. Here she is now, a decade plus deep into the relationship, and that statement still haunts her. And, I get it. It was wrong to say that. That was her moment and someone else fucked it up by what they had to say.

I've known some people who just do not care about what other people think or say. That's probably a good space to operate from. But, most of us are not like that. We hear, we listen, we contemplate what people say. Some things we hear just pass through our field of listening. Some things we hear make us angry. Some things we hear make us happy. Some things we hear make us sad. But, what is the causation factor for all of that? It is what one person is saying.

I have found as I have passed through life, some people are very calculating with what they have to say. They contemplate their words. They choose them very carefully. They do this to help and they do this to hurt. Others, just spout out whatever is on their mind. But, in either case, those words have the same effect in being hurtful or helpful.

Words are power things. They can hurt a person and they can help a person.

How about you? How do you treat the words you speak? Do you allow your emotions to control what you say? If you do, do you realize that your emotions are just your emotions and what gives you the right to spread your emotions onto the life of someone else via your words? Do you possess the ability to chart your words, even if you are emotional, and do you care about the impact that your words may unleash onto the life of someone else?

Life and communication in life is a complicated subject. What you say will be heard by others. It will be interpreted by others. It can help and it can hurt others. Do you have the right to do that? Do you have the right to speak? Do you have the right to not care or to care about what you say?

Do you have the right to affect the life of someone else simply because you have a mind, a mouth, and the ability to speak?

A conscious person is conscious about what they say and what effect what they say will have on others. A negatively calculating or an unconscious person does not possess the ability to care or analyze these variables. They just mindlessly speak, spouting whatever it is they feel, think, or believe. But, is this the right way to operate in life?

In the Free World you can say whatever it is that you want to say. But, if what you say affects someone else, it will also affect you. What you say will be remembered and that is how you will be remembered. What you say will affect the person you are speaking about and it will affect you because you were the one to say it.

You should really think about what you say, how you say it, what you mean by what you say, and what affect what you say will have on someone else.

Consciously calculate your speech because if you don't, what you say, and how what you said affected someone else, may be the only thing that you will be remembered by.

* * *
25/Dec/2018 10:56 AM

Do you think when you dream?

*   *   *

25/Dec/2018 10:55 AM

God can't forgive you for your sins. The only person who can forgive you is the person or persons that you hurt.

Cinematic Enlightenment
21/Dec/2018 07:58 AM

When I discuss filmmaking, and particularly *Zen Filmmaking,* I often reference the term, Cinematic Enlightenment. From this, I often receive the question, *"What is Cinematic Enlightenment?"* I believe for the true filmmaker they already know the answer to that question. But, for the novice or the non-filmmaker, they wonder what I am speaking about. To explain…

As a filmmaker, you are constantly attempting to capture that perfect image. The ideal representation of what you are seeing with your eyes. You want to bring what you are physically viewing, via the pathway of your mind, and capture it in a filming format that then perfectly presents that image to the viewer. This is a process of body, mind, and camera continuum. Much of the time these elements do not come to together to find a perfect harmony. Yes, as a filmmaker, you may adequately capture the image. But, it is only in those moments of interwoven camera, body, and mind perfection that the image is captured perfectly.

For many, in fact most, they do not understand that filmmaking is based in philosophy. They see it simply as a means of entertainment. Thus, a movie is just something that they like or they do not like. Some may even understand that filmmaking is an art form. Most, however, do not comprehend that true, actualized filmmaking is based in the unique philosophy of the individual filmmaker. As each true filmmaker possesses (or at least should possess) their own unique philosophy, this means that they interpret the filmmaking process by their own set of standards and guidelines. Thus, they seek a particular outcome for each scene that they hope to capture with a camera.

Just as in Zen Buddhism we learn that Satori (instantaneous enlightenment) happens in the mind of the individual in a moment of perfect realization, this is the same with Cinematic Enlightenment. It is the perfect combination of combining what the eyes see, with what the mind visualized the scene to be, and then perfectly capturing that scene and ultimately projecting it onto the screen. Thus, Cinematic Enlightenment is the filmmaker finding instantaneous perfection, realized in their own mind, via the medium of eye, camera, and mind coordination.

To conclude, just as it is understood in Zen Buddhism, there is no absolute pathway to achieving Nirvana and there is no one Enlightenment. Enlightenment is realized by the individual in their own unique manner. Thus, there is no school for Cinematic Enlightenment and there are no techniques one has to practice to realize it. It is a natural process that the true filmmaker is allowed to recognize when they let go of their physical aspirations, they remove desire from the filmmaking equation, and they allow their body, mind, eyes, and the camera to form a cohesive unit that establishes a perfect reality that is allowed to harness an image, if only for a moment, and then project that image onto a screen. From this, perfect realization of the outside world blended in coordination with the internal world of the mind's eye is realized and Cinematic Enlightenment is experienced.

Don't Mess With The Teacher's Pet
20/Dec/2018 09:22 AM

Recently, I was told a story by my one friend who works in the corporate nine-to-five work force. Each year, at their place of employment, they get reviewed by their supervisor. My friend's review went fine but the supervisor totally went after and ripped on this other employee—another employee that is totally loved by the big boss. Of course, this person was upset by their review and brought it to the attention of the big boss. BOOM! The supervisor was fired immediately. Don't mess with the teacher's pet.

You know, this really goes to the subject matter of a lot of life and lives. Some people are able to find a position, and for whatever reason, they become loved by the powers that be. Other people, no matter how hard they work, their contribution is never truly appreciated.

I think back to my childhood and a situation that occurred to me that may shed some light on this subject. As a child, I moved a lot. I went to at least ten grammar schools. When I was about eight we moved to this L.A. suburb and I started going to a new school. It was the weirdest experience. An experience I had never encountered before. The teacher hated me. I don't know why. That was back in the period of my life before way too much shit had happened to me and I was actually trying to be a good student. But, if the ball got knocked over the fence, the teacher yelled at me. If two kids got into a fight, a fight I had nothing to do with, the teacher yelled at me. While behaving in this matter to me, I also noticed that she loved this other young boy. He would start a ruckus and she never blamed him. He messed up on his spelling test but she gave him a gold star anyway. It was really weird. I watched. I observed. But, there was nothing I could do to change the game.

I believe in life we all find people that we like and we also find people that we don't like. But, what is the basis for any of this? In most situations, you like somebody because you are attracted to something that they possess. Be it looks, intelligence, a hard work ethic, a promise of something else, or whatever... People like other people. From this, people like people that like the same things that they like. In the adverse, people don't like people they don't like and they don't like people that the people that they like, dislike. Sure, this is the way of life but think how many lives are defined and altered by what and whom one person likes and what and whom one person dislikes.

My assumption is, the aforementioned supervisor was giving his honest opinion about the employee in question. Prior to that I heard they got along fine. But, due to his voicing his opinion it cost him is job a week before Christmas. That's pretty messed up I think. Merry Christmas to him. Was his opinion wrong? How can an opinion be wrong? Plus, part of the job he was hired for was to provide his opinion once a year.

After the supervisor's firing, the employee was immediately promoted to the supervisor's job. This employee, less educated, and a decade or two younger than her associates. Why was she promoted over others? Somebody, a person in the position of power, liked her.

So, here we are, this is life. What can we learn from this story? Only do your job if you don't mess with the teacher's pet.

Rejecting the Responsibility
19/Dec/2018 08:07 AM

Have you ever watched a person as they become deeply involved in a religion? They make statements like, *"I have turned my life over to the lord."* But then, the give and the take begins. *"God has blessed me with this gift."* Or, *"I have given my whole life to the lord why didn't he help me?"*

Of course, all of the soothsayers of the faith have reasons and/or excuses for all of these life happenings in the existence of a person. If something good happens, they explain, *"You need to give thanks."* If something negative happens, *"God is testing you,"* is the common response. *"Just have faith."*

Some, in times of abundance, truly give back to their church and its congregation as they bask in their self-rewardedess. While others, scream at their deity in disbelief over why their life is so cursed. In each of these cases, what is removed from the equation is Self. Namely, a person's own responsibility for the decisions that they made that lead them to a position of abundance or devastation.

Certainly, most of us have, at times, turned our minds towards the heavens seeking divine intervention. If it came, it was appreciated. If it did not, we felt anger and betrayal. None-the-less, it was we, as an individual, who desired a specific outcome to a life event. Thus, it was only we who could appreciate or despise that outcome.

People, who dramatically turn their life over to that abstract supreme power want to gain the promised super power that comes from being in cahoots with god. They want that intangible promise of god's power added to the equation of their life. But, by bringing the supreme power into the calculation, people also remove their own responsibility in any issue. Instead of holding themselves responsible they no longer are the one to blame. It is god's fault, not theirs.

Though this is a common pattern of people who immerse themselves deeply in their religion, it is also a very dangerous mindset to operate from. Not only can the leaders of their religious group easily guide them down a dark path but also, by not seeing themselves as the ultimate causation factor in their life, they remove themselves from the chain of responsibility.

In life, there is really one fact that is very obvious. No matter what you believe, no matter who you believe in, it is you who makes the choices about what you do. Thus, it is only you who is ultimately responsible.

Everybody is Everywhere
but The Truth is Nowhere
18/Dec/2018 07:28 AM

How many people do you know? How many people do you have actual interactive conversations with? How many of those people are you actually face-to-fact with as you interact? How many people do you have interactive conversations with via telephone, texting, on Skype, or on Facetime? How many of those people do you think about after your conversations are done? How many of those people do you speak about to other people? How many of those people do you introduce to other people?

Relationships are defined by the interactive interaction of two or more people. It is the meeting, the greeting, and then the interacting. Some people you meet and you like them. Some people you meet and you become infatuated with. Some people you meet and you are forced to interact with them. Some people you meet and you hate. Some people you meet and you initially like but then as you get to know them better and you no longer like them. Some people you come to never want to interact with again.

Today, in this world, everybody is everywhere. Via the available technology you can communicate, virtually immediately, with people thousands of miles away from you. You can connect with those you like, those you love, those you are interested in, and even those you don't like and want nothing to do with. But, is the person you are connecting with actually who they claim to be. The farther you are from them, the more you are divided by technology, the harder it becomes to judge.

What is all of this interactive consciousness based up? It is based upon what you like, what you don't like, and what you want to receive from another person. It is based upon the human need to bond with other people. But, there is a problem in all of this. There is a problem with who you are and what you portray. There is a problem with who they are and what they portray. There is a problem with the presentation of Self verses the actuality of Self.

Think about it… Have you ever twisted the truth of you, your life, or who and what you are to anyone to make You seem like a bit better version of You? Has anybody ever done that to you? Have you ever lied to another person? Have you ever been lied to? Have you ever presented a persona to the world, something that is based in You but does not present the actual whole essence of You?

Many will say that it is human nature to hide one's flaws and project one's strengths. That may be the case but that is not the actual projection of truth nor is that the emulation of the True Self.

Why do you pretend to be something that you are not? Think about this and come to a definition in your own mind. Why have you hidden who and what you truly are? Why have you lied about who and what you truly are? Why have you projected a false image of yourself to others?

In life, we are all a creation of circumstance, of experience, of personal personality, and of our interactions with other people. But, if a person is not a whole version of themselves, if they are not who they are protecting, who they claim to be, then what are we left with? We are left with a world of communication based upon lies.

Next time you think about altering who and what you truly are to project a false image of yourself; next time you think about lying, care enough to think about the impact that a lie will have on the life of the other person and what that lie will create to the overall evolution of your life and all life.

People may lie to you. You can't control that. People may deceive you as to whom they actually are. You can't control that. But, what you can control is how you embrace the truth of how you project yourself to the world.

Live in a space of truth. Project only the truth. Then, only the truth and the truthful people will find their way into your life.

The more you lie, the more you attract liars. Tell the truth.

I Don't Know What I Was Supposed To Become
14/Dec/2018 12:24 AM

I don't know what I was supposed to become. I didn't come from money. I didn't grow up in a family that was well connected. I was the first person in my family to ever graduate college and then go onto grad school.

I grew up in a very dysfunctional family, long before that term was even coined. I wasn't poor but I grew up in some of the crappies parts of L.A. I had to fight all of the time.

Yeah, I used to walk down Hollywood or Sunset Blvd. on my way to high school everyday. But, if you knew Hollywood in the 70s (and even today) it was and is not a nice place. Yet, I survived.

I have watched as some people have critiqued my life over the years. But, they did not live it. So, they have no true knowledge of who and what I am. Yet, they talk. Some even make money by speaking about me (and other people). I always find that very strange—very disingenuous.

All I ever had was my drive and my ability to attempt to achieve something by working hard to realize it. All there was, was me. Some of the things I hoped to actualize, I did. Others, in fact most, I did not. Yet, I continue to try.

The reason I speak about this is that so many people are trapped by circumstance. So many people are provided with very few options. In fact, many of my contemporaries walked away when they were young. They quit high school. They stopped pursuing their dream. They were forced into the fact of existence.

If you are not one of those people, I have always believed that you should be very thankful.

Thankful for what you did not have to sacrifice. For many people I have known have become none of the things that they hoped they would be. From this, some have become liars. Others have become bitter. Many have become drunks, drug addicts, and the disagreeable. But, all of these things are not what they hoped to become.

I was messing around on the internet a while back and I found the high school yearbook of my mother. There she was in her senior photograph. My father, he went to Manual Arts High School, here in L.A. I looked, but his yearbook is not online. At least not that I could find. Maybe he took a senior photo, maybe he did not. I didn't. By that point in my life I thought that high school was just something I had to do. But, a senior picture, forget about it. My life was focused elsewhere: yoga, music, spirituality.

The thing I thought about when looking at my mother's photo was, there she was all those years ago. What dreams did she have then? What dreams did she achieve? My parents dead—dead, decades ago. I am all that is left of their union. But, what does it all mean? My father died long before he could ever have hopes for me. I was ten years old. My mother, a complicated person, hurt my life more than helped. Yet, I am all that is left. What can it mean? What can anything mean?

So, here we are: you and I. Two people living life; lost in life. We all have our aspirations. We all hope to become. We all hope to do what we want to do. But, how many of us achieve that? How many of us ultimately live the life that we wanted to live?

Life is a complicated subject. I wish I had an answer but I do not.

The Price of Your Emotions
13/Dec/2018 08:32 AM

In *the Tao Te Ching* there is an essential passage that can be translated as, *"In life, three in ten are followers of life, three in ten are followers of death, and three in ten are just passing between life and death."* Add those numbers up and what do you come up with? Nine. What about the tenth person? …I'll get to that in a moment.

Do you ever take the time to study those people around you? Do you ever take the time to study yourself? If you look around, and if you watch closely and study, you will see that some people are very motivated by negativity, while some people are very motivated by positivity. You can see it in the way they behave. Thus, some are followers of life while others are followers of death. For some, the smallest thing will send them into a rage. I mean, look at the posting boards on the internet, that style of person is all over the place. Hidden, they express. But unhidden, they are still who they are. If you are anywhere near them you can see their negativity and anger constantly brewing.

This is the same with people who are very positive. But, the interesting thing I have always noticed about the people who embrace positivity is that they are commonly the ones who are the most silent. They do very little, they just smile. Not that a smile isn't great but the people whom base their existence on this mindset do not seem to the be the ones who are motivated to encounter, confront, and/or interact with others, especially if that other person embraces negativity. Thus, those who base their life upon the negative emotion of anger always seem to have the loudest voice.

Then, there are those who just do not care. Have you ever been around a pot head? I always find them to be a great example as they wake and bake and sit around and talk but unless they are pushed into doing something, they do very little. Now, I realize that is a stereotype but sometimes stereotypes are created for a reason. Whatever the motivating factor for this style of person is, they sit back in life and instead of acting on their dreams, they gel.

In each of these cases, the person who is viewing them from the outside could suggest a change or a rearrange but people are who they are, unless they wish to change, change is not going to happen.

Certainly, the worst and most destructive of these cases is the person who bases their life on anger. As I say over and over again, anger equals bad things. But, look around you, how many people have you encountered that base their life on anger? How about you? Do you?

For each of these mindsets, there is a price to pay. There are life actions that are created and damage that is done. For the more passive and positive cases of these mindsets, namely the person who bases their life on positivity and/or inaction, less negativity is given birth to but all things in life equal something—something that defines a person's life and defines those who are forced into interaction with them.

Understanding this, what do we come away with? What we come away with is that we are left with the one person who is not added to any of those equations. The person who, in *the Tao Te*

Ching, is undescribed—they are the perfect example of Tao. They are the ideal example of living life based in a perfect space of life interaction. As they are the perfect example of Tao, they are free from the constraints that bind all of those who base their life upon emotional and psychological upheaval. They exist in a space of mindful purity.

Is an individual born into this mindset or can they earn it? Yes; both. But, it has to be a conscious choice, a conscious choice that is left to you—you, the life liver.

So, what are you going to do with your life? Are you going to be dominated by the doing, the thinking, and the emotions that you allow to define and control your life? Or, are you going to become something more, a better, more perfect example of human existence?

Like everything else in life, it is your choice. What choice are you going to make?

Check Your Ego
12/Dec/2018 08:36 AM

A few decades back there used to be this expression that people would use when they felt that someone was being too full of themselves, *"Check you ego!"* Basically, it was a method to make the person get out of their own head, their own self-interest, and check back into the reality of the everybody else. But, how many people actually, check their ego? How many people actually get out of their own head? Yes, some people are more conscious, accepting, and caring of others—some people commonly take others into consideration, but most people are locked into their own projection of Self throughout their lifetime.

I mean, think about it... Anyone who wears a uniform is projecting an ego: a cop, a fireman, a serviceman, a basketball player, a businessman, a priest. They are projecting to the world, *"This is what I am."* Isn't that ego? Certainly, some people, in some professions, must wear their uniform but isn't it they who set about on a course to be forced into that uniform?

Then, there are the people who embrace a style. Whether it is a clothing style, a hairstyle, a shoe style, a whatever style; they want to project who and what they are to the world. Though this is very common, isn't this too ego based?

I think back to whom I used to be when I was a teenager very involved in Eastern spirituality. My mother was this master home seamstress. I would buy her some cool material and she would make me these great drawstring yoga-style pants and kurta-style shirts. I was the envy of all my friends in spiritual circles. But, then came punk rock and, embracing the rebellion of the movement, I was torn somewhere between the two. Then, I returned to India and became very disillusioned with all of the formalities of the promised spiritually. Returning to the U.S., via Japan, I shaved my long straggly beard and began to wear sport coats and suits, something I have not changed since. Ego? Or, just a representation of how I see myself and the lifestyle I embrace?

I think back to an episode of Mike Judge's animated TV series, *King of the Hill*. The main character Hank Hill goes into this discussion about *Members Only* jackets and how he thought he would wear one forever. But, times changed and so did he... Funny... You can still see elderly men wearing them sometimes. I always question, how did they keep them that nice for all of these years? And yes, some Hipsters have re-embraced them. But, they were then and this is now. Time and people change.

So, think about this... How do you define yourself? How do you want to be perceived by the world? How much of who you are and how you present yourself to others is defined by where you find yourself in your life and how much of it is defined by whom you truly want to be?

Everybody has an ego. Yes, some people's egos are out of control. I mean, just look at some of the people on Reality TV. It is so easy to see. Even look around you. Maybe you can point out a few. But, if ego is a defining factor of life—if it is something we cannot escape, then it becomes a mental project that we must keep in check if we hope to be a betterment to other people, society, and ourselves.

Be honest, do you allow your ego to control some or all of your actions? Do you allow it to control what you do, how you do it, what you say, and what you think?

The truth be told, if you are not very consciously in control of yourself, your ego can take hold. It can control you. From this, you may be driven down the road to demise via spending too much money on your outward projection onto ruining your face with plastic surgery.

Ego can be a very bad thing if you allow it to control you. Do you?

Some people look outside of themselves and attempt to call out the ego of others, *"Check your ego!"* Though you can easily see a person who is ego driven, it is much harder to look at yourself, define your own inner motivations, and control yourself instead of shifting other people's, and your own, mental focus onto someone else.

Yes, we all have an ego. That is one of the defining factors of human existence. Are you in control of your ego or is your ego in control of you? Only you can answer that question. If your ego is in control of you, what are you going to do about it? Can you be strong enough to take back control? Or, will you allow how you want to be perceived by the world to guide your every action?

moment and that is all they feel. They may be looking forward to the evening when they can go and have a drink, go to the gym, or watch a TV show. They may be looking forward to the weekend when they do not have to go to work. But, that too is locking themselves in their moment. Their moment of now, thinking about what is to come in their life later.

But, what if someone did something to you that stopped you from living your next moment— the next moment you dream of living? How would you feel? What would you feel?

What if you did something to stop someone else from living the next moment they anticipate living? How would you feel? What would you feel? How would you feel about what they feel? Would you even care?

Many/most people lock themselves into a very egocentric mindset of selfishness and denial. They think about themselves. They care about themselves. They may also care about those they love, but this is a very selfish emotion. It is still them thinking about themselves.

People live in denial. They live in denial about what their life actually is. They live in denial about what caused them to arrive at the place in life where they find themselves. They live in denial about what they have done to the lives of other people.

Should you live your life this way? Of course not. You should care. You should chart your existence very consciously. You should chart your existence with regard to all those other people you encounter in life. To gage a person's true aptitude for living an actualized life all you have to do is to view the way they behave—behave in regard to their own life and behave in regard to the way they treat, think about, and speak of other people.

Consciousness is the easiest pathway. But, it is a pathway that very few embrace. Why? Because most people live in denial about who and what they are; who and what they have done; how they got to where they find themselves in life, and what they have done to the life of other people. Most people live in denial. How about you?

* * *

10/Dec/2018 08:16 AM

If you don't find then you are always looking.

* * *

10/Dec/2018 08:12 AM

Some people do nothing but good things.

Some people do nothing but bad things.

Most of us fall somewhere in between.

For every bad thing you do there are consequences.

For every good thing you do there are consequences.

But most people never accept the fact that when they have done something that has hurt someone else when their own instigated negativity comes to find them that they are the one who is actually to blame.

Most People Don't Write An Autobiography
08/Dec/2018 07:50 AM

Most people do not write an autobiography. They do not leave a record of how they felt and why. Most people do not record their feelings for the world to see, contemplate, and remember. They simply feel what they feel, when they feel it, then that emotion is gone. This is not right, this is not wrong, this is simply the way people have lived their life for centuries.

Think about it. How many people know the way you feel. Yes, in certain moments of emotional crisis you may reveal your feeling to your close family or friends but do you tell them everything? Probably not. This is the same with psychotherapy and why it is a flawed science. Yes, you may tell your therapist what you are thinking and feeling but you are filtering what you say to them. You are only telling them only what you want them to hear. Thus, they can only judge your mental state and why you do what you from a very limited self-edited perspective.

As the world has come to embrace social media over the past two decades, there are those who reveal their feelings to the masses. This is especially the case when something has gone wrong with their heath or their relationship. Some speak of the pain or the loss they feel, seeking sympathy and solace. But, those people are a very small percentage of the world masses and the fact is, the most common psychological thread for anyone who reveals their inner self to the unknown masses is that they are an exhibitionist. That's not a judgment, that is simply an observation of fact.

In your life, think about it, your emotions are one of the most driving factors of your existence. What you feel and why you feel it sets the larger definition of your life. Yet, few, if anyone, actually knows what you are feeling and fewer yet even care.

Contemplate this for a moment... Do you care about what someone you do not know is feeling? Do you ever think about what a passing person is emotionally going through as they walk past you on the street? The answer to these questions is most probably, no. Most people are far too locked up in their own set of emotions to ever truly contemplate the joy or the pain someone else is experiencing. Yes, if someone you love is hurting that stirs your emotions. But, are those emotions based in caring what they are feeling or are they simply based upon you caring about what you are feeling? ...What you are feeling in relation to them. That person hurt them so you are mad at that person. That is you feeling. That is not you feeling for them. Moreover, think about the girlfriends or the boyfriends you broke up with. Think about the spouses you cheated on. Think about anyone you have ever hurt. Who were you thinking about, you or them? Were you taking their emotions into consideration?

Most people do not write an autobiography. There is a world of emotions going on all around us constantly—there is a world of actions and deeds done every moment but they go unrecorded; they go unnoticed. They are unknown. You feel what you feel and very few, if anybody, knows or cares what you are feeling and you don't care about them.

Most people do not write an autobiography. There is a reason for this. Most people don't care about what anyone else has done or felt unless it affects them personally. Sad but true. Think about it...

Possibility Verses Probability
07/Dec/2018 10:51 AM

There are two primary defining elements in life: possibility and probability. Yes, there is the possibility but that possibility is defined by the probability. Each person has their dreams, their desires, and what they hope will occur in their life but then there is the reality of what most probably will actually occur.

If you take the time to listen to people you will hear a lot of statements about what a person hopes to become, what they want to become, and what they hope will happen in their life. If you listen to yourself, what do you think about? Most probably, you will spend a certain amount of your time dreaming about what you wish would occur for your life.

There is nothing wrong with this. It is part of the human condition. But, the fact is, most of those possibility will never come to pass as their actualization is not a true probability based upon the reality of the person's life.

This is where aspiration in life becomes a complicated matter. This is particularly the case in this modern era where we are all linked and defined by the internet, and virtually anything can be, at least, marginally realized via this medium. Gone are many of the defining factors that set the standards of excellence for times gone past. Thus, there is at least the possibility that any-body can become any-thing. This being said, all life is based upon actualized doing. And, doing is what many people do not do. There are a million reasons for this, but the reality is, doing takes focused effort and that is what many people do not possess. Moreover, your life is defined by where you find your life. Most people never question, are their aspirations in alignment with what they can actually accomplish? And, what is the price to themselves and to others if they pursue their desired life accomplishment?

From where I was born and grew up and based upon the professions I have followed in my life I have witness so many people holding a dream for what they wished to become but, due to that dream, their life, and in some cases the life of their family and friends, were damaged if not destroyed altogether by them pursing their dream. Yet, the dream is what is promised to us all. But, can that dream be had? Can it be had without life obliteration being set into motion? Obliteration to one's own life and to the life of others. Most people never question this. Most, in fact, do not care. Those who actually possess the drive to achieve their desire simply want what they want and they do not consciously consider the consequences. Thus, they move forward damaging all things in the pathway in the quest of achieving their desired attainment. From this mindset and pathway karma is set into motion.

For many of us in life, we have the opportunity, through time, to witness people achieving what they dreamed of achieving. We watch them climb to the top. In many, if not most of these cases however, these people hurt and took advantage of others in their assent. From this, all kinds of negative feelings and negative retributional energy was given birth to. Thus, they climbed up but they fell down hard. But, it didn't have to be that way. They could have cared and helped others in their assent but their only thought was about themselves and what they desired to achieve. Thus, they gained but eventually they also lost.

What does all of this tell us about life? What does this tell us about the dreams of achievement that we possess? What does this tell us about human nature and the desire of possibility verses probability? First of all, people are who they are—a person is who that person is. A person with a desire is one thing but a person who is willing to wholeheartedly pursue that desire is something else. Due to their single-mindedness, their focus is generally solely on themselves. Thus, all others be damned. Now, you can tell a person with this mindset that they should not behave in this manner, you can warn them of the consequences but will they listen? Probably not. At least not until it is too late. Too late and they have hurt others in their assent which eventually comes back to hurt themselves. And, it is from this singular sourcepoint where the damage for the possibility verse the probability of achievement is set into motion.

If a person finds themselves in the right physical, material, and mental atmosphere they can move towards their dreams. If they do this with a conscious mind set towards the better of all, they can achieve without damage. But, the moment this focus is lost, the moment the caring about the other individual is forgotten, then any achievement is doomed for failure. Any step forward will eventually equal a step backward.

In life there is possibility and there is probably. Take a look at your life. What do you desire? What are you doing about what you desire? Now ask yourself, what did you desire one year, five years, or ten years ago? Did you set about on a course of achievement? What did it cost you? What did it cost others? Or, did it cost nothing because you never even tried?

In life, there is always a price to pay for anything/everything. If you are not conscious of that price, that price always becomes too high.

You can look at your life and only desire things for you. You can look at the life of others and include the all and the everyone in the equation. But, if you do not based your doing upon your defined reality everything you do becomes no more than nothing and your probability cancels out your possibility.

Opportunities and What You Do For Others
06/Dec/2018 07:16 AM

Today, what are you going to do for someone else that opens up the door of opportunity for them? What actions are you going to take that allows someone else to become something that they hope to become?

The fact is, most people never even consider what they are going to do for someone else. Yes, if they like someone or they love someone they may perform actions that bring the two of them closer together. But, that is not giving, that is taking. Yes, they may dislike or be angry with someone so they attempt to hurt their life. But again, that is a self-fulfilling action. That is not giving. That is not caring. But, few set about on a course that will actually provide opportunities for someone else to grow and become. How about you? What do you do for others to help them become what they hope to be?

Think about something that you wanted to become earlier in your life. Who, if anyone, helped you obtained that goal? How do you feel about that person? For most, they feel fairly indebted for if they had not been given that helping hand they may never have become.

Think about something that you wanted to become earlier in your life—something that you did not become. Why didn't you achieve your goal? Most probably, you did not become because no one opened the door for you and helped you achieve what you hoped to achieve.

Each person, in his or her life, wants to become something. These something's change over time. But, becoming is the goal. Without help, however, becoming can become very complicated if not impossible.

Each person, at every stage of their life, has the ability to help someone else. You are something—whether that something is small or large is unimportant. But, you can help someone. You can allow them to live their dream. What are you going to do?

For me, as a filmmaker, I was always happy to help actors and actresses achieve their dream of being on the screen. That is why I so often worked with unknown talent. For me, as a martial arts instructor, that is why I was so happy to train budding practitioners. I hoped to guide them towards their physical, mental, and self-defense goals. And, by the way, for all of the years I professionally taught the martial arts, I did it for free, and I still do.

Everybody wants to become something. What are you going to do today that will help them achieve that dream?

You Don't Understand
04/Dec/2018 11:19 AM

Have you ever been in one of those situations where you are attempting to communicate something to a person and it becomes quite clear that they just do not understand? I imagine that most of us have felt that way at one time or another. Certainly, this is a common occurrence between parents and children, particularly in the rapidly ever-changing world that we find ourselves currently living in. But, that is almost expected. This situation becomes more perplexing when you and another person of a similar age and cultural make up find that you exist in two very separate spaces of understanding. Is one right? Is the other wrong? Or, are you simply basing your life on a different set of life experiences?

As a filmmaker, I have run into this situation more than a few times on a professional and a non-professional level. This has occurred most commonly with people who are not an active part of the filmmaking industry. There is one fact that I came to understand very early on in my emersion into the film business and that fact is, if you are not an active part of the industry you can have no clear understanding of what takes place in the industry. Sure, you can have your opinions. But, an opinion is not based in fact. An opinion is based in a preconceived bias. And, an opinion is very different from a factual understanding.

Now, I use the film industry as an example because I am so closely tied to it. I could also reference the music business, the publishing industry, the world of martial arts, or really any other field. There are the people who are actually involved in it and then there are the people who see if from the outside looking in—thinking they know but they can never know because they have no actually interpersonal experience.

The working environment is one thing but the life environment is something else. Here, you find people who see life and life events completely different from one another. You may see it one way, they may see it another. You think you are right and they are wrong. But, they probably think that they are right and you are wrong. But, who is right? And, why do people interpret life differently?

On one hand there is no easy answer to this question but on the other hand the answer is, in fact, very easy. People view life via their individual life indoctrination. They do what they do based upon how they were trained to react.

Many freethinkers, particularly in the cultural revolution that took place in the 1960s, began to exclaim that people should stop allowing themselves to be programmed. To stop believing what they hear. To remove themselves from their parental programing. To do their own thing. This was not a bad ideology as it allowed those people, with an open mind, to attempt to step back from the way they were trained to behave. But, this free thinking mindset quickly shifted from modern consciousness as the, *"Me Generation,"* took hold and people wanted money and things instead of enlightenment.

The fact of the matter is, no matter how far you can mentally step away, you are your created by your parental and societal programming—you are still a product of that indoctrination. Some people call it brain washing while others just understand that it is the condition of life. But, no matter by what name you label it, you were programmed to encounter life is a specific manner and very few people posses the mental fortitude to be strong enough to define their own mind and reality. In fact, if you desire to do so and you possess the mental focus you can trace back any of your bad, judgmental, defamatory, or unstable emotional traits and behaviors to one incident that happened to you in your life either at the hands of your family or your peers. Thus, you were created. Very few can claim to be wholly self created. If they do, that is most likely just them speaking from a space of denial-based ego.

So, here we are. You think one thing and I think another. What can we do? In most cases, these differences are minor because people tend to only choose to associate with those of like mind. But, others are forced into our existence from time to time. Other, who do not share our same definitions. Thus, there will be disagreements.

To answer, the conscious person allows another person be who they are and believe what they believe. The unconscious, self-righteous, dominate person, however, attempts to shift others to their system of belief. But, this is simply based in ego. *"I know more than you."*

Mostly, disagreements lead to bad things. Disagreements lead to wars. Can you be strong enough in yourself to allow another person to believe what they believe even if you don't believe it? Can you be strong enough not to judge? Can you be clear enough, in your own self-reality, to allow others to think what they think without desiring to change their mind? If you can, you walk the path towards self-realization. If you can't, you walk the road of ego and a mindset defined by someone else though you are most likely not clear enough to trace that influence to its source and take control over it.

* * *

04/Dec/2018 10:39 AM

If you are unhappy with your life you are always looking for a reason to criticize someone else.

The Darkness Behind the Veil
02/Dec/2018 07:55 AM

For each of us there is some dark something that we wish to keep hidden from the rest of the world. This list of what these dark something's are can be virtually endless but the common ones are personal behavior flaws, actions we committed once and we wish that we did not, things that happened to us that are very embarrassing, or something that was forced onto us that we did not desire. These elements of darkness are in our remembered subconscious; we know them but we wish that the rest of the world never hears about them.

Some people tell no one of these dark something's. In some cases, people speak of these things only to close family or friends. Some only talk about them to their shrinks or their priests. Some let elements of these situations slip out by accident while there are a few that blurt them out to the world as if it is somehow a badge of honor—the honor of being damaged. But, those people are very few.

Commonly, there is a subgroup of people who takes pride in knowing the flaws of someone else. They were not knowingly made privy to this knowledge but by some unexpected or devious means they came by this information. Then, they either use it against the person via threats or by constantly reminding them of something that they do not wish to think of. From this, that outside person gains a misguided sense of power over the individual.

The fact is, the person who does something like this is a very low-minded individual. They prefer to cast the darkness outside of themselves, calling out the flaws of others, so people will not look too closely at their own inadequacies or darkness.

In our lives, each of us has some or many of these dark hidden secrets. Some have been more fortunate than others and they do not have much to hide. That's great. But, the fact is, we all have something buried deep in our mind—something lived in our past that we wish did not happen, we wish we could have controlled, and we wish no one else would ever know about.

The answer? There is none. Every person has a different answer. Each person who practices a different religion or a different psychology will tell you something different to do. In the end, this is just life, you will be hurt, you will be embarrassed, you will do bad things. All you can do is to be as conscious and in control of your own mind, actions, and life as you can be. Don't hurt people, be kind to people, be compassionate, don't do things that you will later regret, and try to be forgiving of yourself for the bad choices that you made in the past. The best way to achieve all of this. Only do good, kind, and honorable things. Don't hide behind your veil of darkness simple let it fade from your consciousness.

Thought Without Thought
27/Nov/2018 07:27 AM

When one studies the meditative mind, one is continually embraced with the concept of No Thought. No Thought is the purpose of meditation, as it is understood when one is able to freeze their thought patterns True Self or Cosmic Self may be encountered.

In the modern era, the various practices of meditation have come to be embraced on a much larger worldwide scale than ever before. Look around you, how many people are practicing one form of yoga or another. It fact, yoga is very prominent across the entire western marketplace. What has occurred from this, however, is a dumbing down of yoga, its true essence, and the foundational elements of what actually makes up its elemental philosophy. Ask the average person why they practice yoga and you will hear many answers, most of which involve Personal Self. *"It makes me feel calm." "It helps me lose weight." "It gets me to my center,"* and so on. But, ask a modern practice about the spiritual essence of yoga—ask them do they understand that the term, *"Yoga,"* is actually translated as, *"Union," "Union with god,"* and the majorly of the modern practitioners will either not know this fact or will immediately claim, *"That is not why I do it."* From this fact alone, it is obvious that the essence of yoga is lost.

Hand-in-hand with the fact that most people do not understand what yoga truly is, the modern teachers of yoga have lost track of one of the primary elemental factors to the true practice of yoga; namely meditation.

Mediation is taught in virtually all courses on yoga. After the physical exercises, the instructors commonly run their students through a few pranayama, breath control techniques, and then guide them into meditation, describing its benefits. But, is the true essence of meditation being taught? No. More often than not people are told to not worry about the fact that their mind will wander and to just bring it back to its center. Then, after a few moments of attempted mental silence, as the cars drive past outside, class is over, hugs are giving, and that is that. Is that yoga? Is that meditation? Does that lead to the Thoughtless Mind? No.

The problem with this entire process, and how it not only describes the way the majority of the populous of the world commonly behaves, but it also details how modern teachers feed into all of the world unconscious unconsciousness in that people are given an ancient practice defined by modern excuses. They are taught what they believe is a pathway to better body and mind. Believing that they are doing a good thing, they do not become any more whole or better from a spiritual perspective. Thus, though their bodies may feel better, no better Self is encountered.

Think of all the individuals you have met that are not very nice people; yet they practice yoga? If you live in a large city, where power, money and ego reigns supreme, there may be a vast amount of people you know like this. Yet, they claim to be practitioners of yoga. Are they?

This takes us to the ultimate definition of Mind Science. This takes us to the essence of whom a human being is or is not. This takes us to the sourcepoint of why we do anything. As yourself, *"Why do you do what you do?" "Do you know why you do what you do or do you just do?" "Do you do based in an evolved sense of human betterment or do you do based in anger, fear, greed, or desire?"* For most, they are guided by the Reactive Mind and they do not even question what they do what they do or why they are going to do it before they do. They just get an idea and they do. But, from this, look at all life—this is how life damage on a personal and a global scale is instigated. This is the Unthinking Mind.

Now, back to the original premise of their piece, the pursuit of No Thought. What is the different between No Thought and the Unthinking Mind? In simple terms, No Thought is based on the advanced understanding of a conscious pathway to Mind Silence. However, the Unthinking Mind is based on Reactive Consciousness driven by human desire. Thus, the two have similar names but entirely different life applications.

What does this explain to us about life? It allows us to understand that as long as something is outside of ourselves; whether it is being taught as something as seemingly spiritual as yoga or purely self-driven like all of the life actions based upon all of the Mind Stuff of modern humanity, unless a mind has a focus on the essence of Being their can be no True Knowledge gained from yoga or anything else. In fact, all that is born is simply ongoing karma, retributions, and reactions.

Silence your mind and the essence of Life and Self is understood. Look outside of yourself for anything, even spiritual training, and nothing but altered borrowed knowledge is given birth to which sets all life catastrophes into motion.

* * *
27/Nov/2018 06:42 AM

If you want to know who a person truly is, look in their closet.

* * *

26/Nov/2018 05:05 PM

How often do you not notice what is right in front of you?

*   *   *

26/Nov/2018 04:57 PM

You can't undo what you've done in the past so you should make your decisions with your eyes on the future.

* * *

25/Nov/2018 02:13 PM

It is easy to lie when nobody knows the truth.

Life Is Only Lived In Your Mind
25/Nov/2018 07:22 AM

Have you ever had the experience of remember something that you did sometime ago with another person. You get together with that person some time later and you begin to verbally reminisce about what took place. The only noticeable thing is, they remember the situation somewhat differently from you. Maybe their memory is vastly different from yours, maybe it is only a few minor details, but you both were there, you both lived the experienced, but, their memory of what took place is different from yours. How can this be?

The reason these type of situations take place is that each person processes a life experience differently. They come to each situation with a different set of life definitions. From this, they mentally process, and thereby remember, each life encounter in a different way.

This is just a very obvious example of the fact that people live life in their own mind. But, this life fact guides us forward from this point.

Think about a time somebody hurt you. You did not want that to happen. You did not expect that to happen. Yet, somebody did something that caused you physical or emotional pain. You were both intertwined in the same life situation but you hurt and they did not.

This example can be broken down in a deeper understanding of life reality from this point. Why did they do it? There can obviously be many psychological reasons for their actions but it all comes down to one primary element, they are not you. They live their life from their own perspective.

They do not feel what you feel. Thus, they live their life based upon their own mental understanding about what is appropriate and what is an acceptable life action.

Now, turn this around. Think of someone you hurt. Why did you do it? Were you thinking about them, their life, their emotions, and/or the impact of what you are doing on their existence? Or, where you simply feeling that you have the right, you have the desire, you have the power to do what you do? You are not them. You may be thinking for them but you are not thinking about them. You are living your life based upon your own mental reality. And, your reality is not their reality. Thus, you did what you did. You felt one thing but they felt something very different.

So far, these are very obvious examples of how people live life in their own mind. It can become much more metaphysical from this point.

Your dreams… Who dreams them? You do. Do they affect anyone else? No. Only you.

Your fantasies… Who fantasies them? You do. Do they affect anyone else? No. Only you.

This is where the entire concept of making a fantasy a reality comes into play, particularly in New Age circles. Many a New Age teacher speaks of the ability to make a fantasy a reality simply by focusing very hard on that fantasy and believing it one-hundred percent. Have you ever tried this? How did it work out?

Prayer is also said to be able to achieve this end goal.

The fact is, if you have a dream, which was born in your mind, and you work towards obtaining it, both via your fantasies and your physical hard work, things can be brought from your mind into reality. But, your mind is only your mind and if you do not take physical action to achieve your dream your thoughts cannot make fantasy become a reality.

This is where the secondary element of fantasied reality comes into play; namely the other person. Most fantasies involve other people. Whether it is the fantasy of love, hate, or achievement in a particular field, most hopes involve other people. The thing is, those other people have their hopes, dreams, and fantasies, as well. If your fantasy does not coincide with theirs, there becomes conflict and just as two people remember the same situation somewhat differently, if two or more people do not share the same goal, achievement of anything becomes very difficult.

From a much deeper supernatural perspective, this is why the entire concept of time travel or astral projection is emulated solely from the individual mind. Yes, there are methods to achieve these end goals but where do these desirous mind trips emulate from? The answer, one person desiring to do one thing. Thus, though it can take place; where does it take place? It takes placed in the mind of one person. Thus, any occurrences that may occur from these advanced mental techniques are solely defined in the mind of that one person and, therefore, they cannot be charted in physical reality. So, did they even occur?

Your life is lived by what you experience and what you do. What you do equals your karma. Your karma is your karma based upon the actions you unleash based upon what you envisioned in your mind. Yes, as you pass through life, you may have interactive experience(s), you may, at times, find a group consciousness. But, at the heart of all reality is your reality. You thought it, you lived it, and you did what you did base upon what was formed in your mind. Your life was defined by those thoughts and your actions were unleashed by what you decided to do based upon what was emulating from your mind. Combine that by what you feel about what others have done to you based upon what they were personally thinking and feeling and you can easily see that life is based upon actions unleashed by personal thoughts.

Though what you do may affect other people, just as what other people do may affect you, your life is only lived in your mind.

* * *

24/Nov/2018 07:56 AM

Have you ever had somebody do something really messed up to your life and years later they said, *"I'm sorry."*

What did that change?

Did that undo the damage?

Most people never even care enough to say that they are sorry. But, for those who do, wouldn't it have just been better to not hurt another person's life in the first place?

* * *

23/Nov/2018 05:59 PM

There is always some excuse for why you don't do what you don't do.

There is always some justification for why you do what you do.

The Art That You Don't Create
23/Nov/2018 07:00 AM

It was thanksgiving yesterday and I was at a family function. Not my family. I don't have any blood relatives. At least none that I know of. It was the family of my lady.

In any case, I was speaking to this one young woman who I've know since her birth. I always thought she was a great person. Anyway, she has recently graduated from art school and has come back home to live with her parents. Worried of her acquired student debt, she has taken a job as a waitress. I asked her if she was creating any art and she said that she was not. …That her job took a lot of her time and her energy. My suggestion was that she quit the job and focus on her art. But, she apparently is one of those very financial conscious individuals and said that she must keep working.

I always find this very sad when a person looses their art—whatever that art may be. I mean, every poet wants to become as successful as Bukowski, every filmmaker as successful as Tarantino, every novelist as successful as Stephen King, every musician as successful as Beethoven, and every painter as successful as Picasso. But, that's probably not going to happen. It's one in a trillion that anything like that will happen for. But, that does not mean that you can't continue to create your art at your own level of doing.

I cannot tell how many people I have watched walk down the road of this young lady and take a job but in doing so they lose their art. I think that is very sad.

Yes, if you plan to make a living from your art you are probably going to starve. But, that does not mean that you cannot do something to create an income and still focus on the art that you love. The art that you live for.

A lot people—the people who are not artists, don't get it. They will always question the motivation of an artist. They may say, *"How is that art?"* Or, *"Anybody can do that."* Or question, *"Does that pay your rent?"* But, all that doesn't matter. They don't get it. They will never understand, because art and being an artist is not a part of their psychological makeup. But, for those who are artists, that should be the focus of their life. They should never let that go.

In any case, I'm told that I can be a little intense when I'm passionate about a subject and I guess I was that way with this young lady. I don't mean to be intense. But, that's just how I come off. So, I'm guessing I put her off a little bit. But, it was all out of love. Love of the art.

You know, I've talked a lot about this in the past but I will see people's discarded art all over the place: thrift stores, flea markets, even in the garbage. I think that's sad that someone created something and then it is cared about no longer. But, at least they created it. They had the dedication and the focus to do it. How can you criticize that?

So, if you're an artist, whatever that art may be, don't lose your art. Don't let the world take away your art. For without art, we, as the human culture, possess very little. Love art. Live art.

*   *   *
20/Nov/2018 08:30 AM

Is what you're doing worth your doing?

The Rank That You Earn
19/Nov/2018 08:39 AM

In regard to the martial arts, like I have long said, *"If you are referring to yourself as a master, that problems means that you are not."*

I understand that people want position in life. Whether it is martial art rank, job title, or number of follows on Instagram or Twitter, people want to feel as if they are something and appear as if they have achieved something. This has lead people to pursue all kinds of pathways to gain a place in society where they can claim that they are, *"A Something."* Some of these pathways have been based on hard work. Other of these pathways have been based upon cooking the books. But, one way or the other, certain people strive towards titling.

But, what does it mean when you get there? What do you do with your position of title equaling power? Do you unleash good or do you unleash harm? Or, is where you have arrived simply a place where your ego is allowed to be stroked?

As I have long tried to explain to people, the term, *"Master,"* most commonly used with the Korean martial arts, (Sabumnim in Korean), is not well-translated into American English. It is much more akin to Old British English where a school instructor was sometimes called, *"Master,"* in reference to him being the head of the class. In modern times, the term, *"Master,"* in association with the martial arts, has come to denote what a person is, *"A Master of the Art."* But, are they? Yes, they may have earned rank, either through years of training or purchase, but look at the people who use this term, are they truly a Master? Do they perform every technique perfectly every time? I have watch ballerinas; some of them are masters. I have watched performers in shows like Cirque du Soleil; some of them are masters. But, is some chubby guy teaching a few students at a small martial art studio deserving of this title? I guess that is a personal decision. But, I have always preferred the Japanese term, *"Sensei,"* which means teacher. But, people want more. They don't want to just be a teacher. They want to be something grand.

The reason I bring this subject up is that I was asked a little while back why I am not a 9th Degree Black Belt as I have been an 8th Degree Black Belt for so long. First of all, I don't care about any of that. But, as I explained, I was offered that rank a number of years ago but I turned it down. Then, the other day, I was going through some papers and I found the letter where the head of the organization offered me the advancement. It was dated 2006. Wow! That was a long time ago. I didn't even realize how long ago that was. Now, even the founder and the head of that organization has passed on.

In any case, I'm not about what I claim to be. I'm not about title. I'm not about presenting an image to the world. I'm just about me being me. I'm about helping and I don't care about the title I am given as I am helping. Just call me Scott.

The problem with the world is... The problem with some people is... (At least as I see it). Instead of working towards being a helpful version of themselves, they first seek to be a something. They want the title. They expect the respect. Whether a person has truly earned any title they use is forever debatable. But, that is not even the point. If you throw away the title, who are they—who are you? If you throw away the number of followers you have on Instagram or Twitter, who are you? If you are alone and yourself who are you?

People who seek titling, often times get lost in that title. Whether it is in martial arts, at the job, or on the web, people become lost in the projection of who they appear to be. But, who are they really? Are they that title? Or, are they person who is below that title? The person who's life is only known to a very few (or no one)?

If you are nothing... If you seek to be nothing... Then titling has no hold on you. You can give, you can help, but by claiming the freedom of being nothing you are not bound by what any title describes you to be. Thus, all that you do is done from the space of purity.

Now, I get it... Most people want to be that, *"Something."* But, even if that is you, try letting go for a minute. Stop allowing others to refer to you as a something. Stop describing yourself, in your own mind, as that something. How freeing is that?

Let go of titling and you can be anything. Plus, you can be it in the purist sense of the word. As you are nothing... As you claim nothing... You can give everything. And, giving/helping, without taking, (without your ego being stroked), that is the best thing you can do with your life.

Let go of your desire to be a something. Then you are free. Then you can truly help.

* * *
19/Nov/2018 08:38 AM

Everything is open to interpretation.

What You Were Then You Are Not Now
16/Nov/2018 08:22 AM

The one constant fact about living life is that you change, you evolve, you grow, and you become a different person based upon a defining set of parameters that you hold deeply within your spirit. Is who you are today, who you were one year or ten years ago?

The older you get the more experiences you encounter and the possibly for you to evolve expands. This being stated, some people find a definition of themselves and they change very little. Through time, experience, and human interactions they hold fast to a very limited definition of themselves. They shun all that is new and different and they refuse to allow the who and the what they are to expand.

Some hold onto a good self. They are a good, kind, helpful, and caring person who is constantly seeking to do positive things. It is hard to find fault with this type of person who, based in goodness, changes very little as they pass through life. Then, there is the other side of this coin. The person who is mean spirited, hurtful, vengeful, deceitful, untruthful, judgmental, vain, egotistical, ager-driven, and destructive. Look at life. Look at people. There is also this style of person who refuses to evolve, as well. Though they may encounter time, age, experience, cultural and emotional interactions, they hold fast to a personality that is not conducive to the betterment of anything. At the end of their days, what have they done that has made anything any better?

Most people fall somewhere in-between these two extreme categories. They are not all-good or all-bad. They move through life and learn through experience but they hold fast to the I that they believe their I is. They are who they are. Not bad, not good, but focused on self.

This is what brings us to the definition of an evolved person. The person who changes through time, as we all do, but does so with the understanding that there are things to learn from the outside world, there are things to gain from each personal encounter, and that by being open to learning from life events they are willing to change who they are, learn from their mistakes, and evolve into a better version of themselves.

How many people do that? Do you? Do you study your life? Do you watch each personal interaction? Do you learn from the way other people behave? Do you learn from how you treat other people? Are you willing to view what you have done and see that action as either a positive or negative contribution to life, people, and life-evolution. Do you realize that you too make mistakes? Do you try to fix any hurtful mistakes you have made? Are you willing to examine the way you behave and evolve into a better version of yourself?

With age comes the perspective of time. Age allows you to look back over a period of time and study what you were then, compared to whom you've become now. It allows you to see that at one point you did one thing, then you stopped and you started doing something else. Ask yourself, why did you stop doing that and start doing this? Was it a conscious choice or was it a forced movement?

Each of us, whether consciously or not, passes through our life. Each of us, whether desiring to do so or not, changes as we pass through our life.

But, it is the consciously conscious person who allows themselves to learn from life and thereby become the better version of themselves.

Do you study your life? Do you look in the mirror of your life? Do you look to the pain you have caused or do you only focus on the joy you have given others which, from their jubilation, has given you joy? Do you study your ego and question why you do what you do? Do you care? Do you allow yourself to become the better more caring you? Do you evolve?

Life can be a great experiment of helpful, positive actions leading to an evolving expansive mind; conscience and helpful to others. It can also be a dark pathway defined only by holding yourself to one place and not caring about others. Which life path do you follow?

Do you evolve? Do you care to evolve?

Mad For What Reason Why?
15/Nov/2018 07:47 AM

Kind of picking up from the previous blog, do you ever study yourself when you get mad? Do you ever go down deep and analyze why you are feeling the feeling you are feeling? Do you ever question your emotions at all or do you just allow your mind to react?

Anger is one of the most destructive emotions that defines the human race. Anger causes people to do all kinds of bad things. Yet, think about it, how much of a person's life is defined by anger? How much anger have you seen? How much of your own anger have you allowed to guide you in what you have chosen to do?

What causes anger? Basically, someone has done something that someone else does not like. Okay… What that means is that there are two variables in that equation. One is the person who is doing the doing and the second is the person who is reacting to the doing.

From a metaphysical perspective, it has long been said that one should not let another person take control over them—that one should not react to what someone else has done. Sure, that is a great and enlightened mindset to operate from. But, for most, that is not always obtainable. Why? For one, most people do not possess that level of control over their emotions. Thus, they react to what is done to them. This is not a bad thing. In fact, it's natural. But yes, when you become angry with someone or something you are allowing that person's actions to take control over your mind and your life. Is that what you want?

This understanding is something you need to think about the next time you find yourself becoming angry with someone. Question, does what they have done actually allow them right to take control over your emotions? I mean, think about it, how many people say bad things and do bad things simply to evoke anger in another person? Are they aware they are doing this? Some are, some aren't. But, nonetheless they are doing it. Thus, motivating anger in another person can be as easy as speaking a few words. Does an unconscious or wrongly self-motivate person have the right to take control over your life and cause you to react?

I believe that all of us can look back to times when someone has done something that has made us angry. But, in the moment of that anger, did you analyze that anger? Did what that person do actually affect your life in just that specific moment or over the long-term? Or, where you mad because somebody did something to someone else? Did what they do actually change the direction of your life? Or, was it just some small mistake that you allowed to take control over your mind?

Think about how anger spreads in the world. One person is mad and other people join in. In some cases, those outside people become more angrily reactive than the person themselves. How is that healthy on any level? Though anger is a highly adrenaline driven reactive emotion, (and it makes some people feel alive), but what it leads to is only pain causing damage. How does that help anyone?

To come to an understanding of anger, you have to trace anger to its roots. Think about a time when you made someone angry. What did you do that made them react? Do you ever question that?

The fact is, though most people will claim all kinds of excuses and justifications for what they do, it always comes down to one person choosing to do one thing that made that other person angry because that one thing hurt that person emotionally or damaged their life materially or physically. So yes, they did do something wrong. Whether they meant to do that or not is debatable but they did it and thus they instigated the anger. It is their fault.

Many wrongs that equal anger are done by mistake. We all sometimes say things without thinking. We all say things that may be meant as a joke but they are taken the wrong way. Accidental words are one thing. They need to be analyzed and their true intention understood. But, then there is the other kind of words. Words that are designed to intentionally hurt a person. Those are just wrong. Those are instigated by a person who does not care about the other person or does not see that other person as a human being. Maybe, they are actually trying to hurt that other person. Do you like to be hurt? Probably not. Thus, intentionally hurting someone, on all levels is just wrong. You should never allow yourself or others, on your behalf, to instigate that style of life-action because all it can do is to generate future anger that leads to more damage and more destruction.

Here are the facts; everyone feels anger. It is virtually impossible to pass through life without someone doing something to you that causes you to feel anger. But, it is you who can stop that trend at its source. Be the person who cares about the other person. Be the person who attempts to understand the other person. If you feel anger in yourself, catch it and control it. If you hurts someone, do all that you can to fix the damage. If you see anger brewing outside of yourself in others, catch it and take control over it. Take hold and guide that negative emotion into the realms of the positive. Say something nice or do something nice so that any anger may be dissipated and replaced with happiness.

Looking for Somebody to Hate
14/Nov/2018 01:51 PM

I was on Facebook today and I noticed that this guy had written a piece completely bagging Mother Teresa. I mean, he really went after her. People were chiming in with comments like, *"Fuck Mother Teresa."* I mean, how messed up is that?

Mother Teresa passed away in 1997. She was canonized in 2016. Was she a perfect person? No. No one is. But, having met her and having volunteered at her clinic in Calcutta a few times I can say, based in her faith, she truly tried to help those sick, dying, and in need.

I think what most people do not understand is that Calcutta is hell. As is much of urban India. Sure, India has some more than beautiful locations and beautiful people but as I have said a million times, India is one of the most violent places on earth and the poverty level is insane. For those who are impoverished in India there is little or no hope. And, those were the type of people Mother Theresa was helping.

But, more to the point, at least in regard to this essay; why does that guy even care about Mother Teresa? She has been dead over twenty years and what she did in no way affected him or the people who were hating on her with their comments. What does it prove to go after someone who is no longer alive? In fact, why go after anyone for any reason when you have no personal interactive knowledge about who or what they truly are and/or why they do what they do or did what they did? Secondhand knowledge is not knowledge at all.

The fact is, some people are at such a low level of human consciousness that they look for someone to hate. For that guy, today it was Mother Teresa, tomorrow it will be someone else. But, what does hating prove? Does it help the impoverished in India? No. It does absolutely nothing but hurt someone else. Hating is bad!

So, this is just some food for thought for you… Next time you hear someone spouting judgment or hate do not let yourself get dragged into his or her frame of mind. In fact, take a look at them and question why are they saying something so judgmental and hate filled in the first place. By doing this, you will most likely be able to see into their true character.

Don't believe what the judgmental or hate-filled speak. When you encounter judgmental hate speak you have one of two positive options. Turn away and don't listen to them or you can say something positive. Though, the truth be told, most people who are locked into a mindset of judgment based in hate don't want to hear anything positive but by saying it you may shift the context of the conversation which may protect others from being dragged into the realm of hate.

Choose love, never hate. Choose to help, never hurt.

You Can't Find What Isn't There
13/Nov/2018 12:54 PM

I had a few minutes so I stopped into this thrift store. ...You never know what you will find... I was walking around and I went over to the sport coat section and was looking through them. I noticed that there was this very large African-American man trying on the blazers. He looked over at me, *"You're bigger than me, you're not going to find anything here."*

His comment struck me as strange as I would guess him to be a couple of inches taller than me, maybe 6'4" or 6'5" and about a hundred pounds heavier. I would describe him as a big burly guy. *"No way,"* I replied, *"You're a big guy."* Yet, in his mind, he saw something that wasn't there.

Post a few more niceties; I noticed that he was going through the coats trying a lot of them on. I mean, this guy was a big guy. If he were at a Big and Tall Store I'm sure he could have found a sport coat. Me, I wear a 48 Long. I would guess him to be a 54 Long or larger. Those are hard to come by in a thrift store as people that size don't generally wear suits and then donate them. Occasionally, he had a coat on and he would asked me what I thought. But, they were all way too small.

Anyway, I wished him, *"Good luck,"* and walked away. There he remained, looking for a sport coat that fit. Trying them on, one by one. Attempting to find a jacket he would never find.

You know, this is a lot how life is and a lot how people behave. They continue to look for something that is not there. They do it with their family, in their personal relationships, in their job, in their dreams of wanting more from a particular person who does not reciprocate their emotions. I have seen this so many times in life. People waste their years, hoping that something will change, that something new will emerge, but nothing will change as what they are looking for, in a place or in a person, it just does not exist.

So, this is just a little food for thought as you pass through your life... Question, and be honest with yourself, can you actually get what you are looking for, where you are looking for it or not? Can you get what you want from the person you hope will give it to you or not? If not, there is no reason to waste your Life Time believing that it will magically appear when what you are looking for does not exist—at least not in the location where you are looking for it.

* * *

13/Nov/2018 12:26 PM

Every step you take gets you farther away from where you started.

* * *

13/Nov/2018 12:25 PM

With some people, if you don't tell them that they've done something wrong they don't realize that they've done something wrong.

If you tell them they've done something wrong and they don't care, that lets you know what type of a person they truly are.

Zen Filmmaking: Process Verse Product
12/Nov/2018 08:36 AM

Here's a piece that I wrote several years ago that you may find interesting.

It seems that there is no way that I can ever discuss *Zen Filmmaking* without speaking about Donald G. Jackson. And, that is not bad thing for without him having the deal in place for *Roller Blade Seven* I may never have come up with the philosophic ideology for the process and continued forward with making Zen Films.

After Don's passing, I was helping his wife clear out some of the tons of things Don had collected—as she and their daughter were moving from the house they had lived in for over twenty years. Don was a terrible hoarder. (Oh, I mean collector. ☺) In any case, as we were going through some stuff we found something that referenced *Zen Filmmaking*. She handed it to me and said, *"I guess this is for you, as you're the source."* I smiled, *"That's me..."*

But, it is much more complicated than that. *Zen Filmmaking* really goes to the source and the difference between who Don and I were as human beings. Don was very explosive, egocentric, a total power tripper, and he did not care about people; their feelings or their thoughts. Though he did spend a lot of money on his young wanta-be starlet paramours getting them boob jobs, paying their rent, and stuff. His payment was retuned by... Well, you can figure that out...

Anyway, working with Don was always both a blessing and a curse. On one hand he was a total hustler, so we had some high budgets for our films. In fact, on one of the last big galas before he died, *Demon Lover Diary* showed at the Directors Guild of America here in L.A. I thought that was a great blessing from the beyond as Don got a lot of press surrounding that event and this happened as he was getting very sick and closely approaching the end of his life—though I and his direct family were the only ones who knew this. After the screening they asked Don to do a Q&A. One of things he said to describe himself, when being asked a question, was, *"I used to be an artist, now I'm just a guy who asks other people for money."* Sad but true.

And, I guess that leads to the point of this piece. Yes, Don was a filmmaker. And, I believe a truly revolutionary and artistic one. But, he was more into the process than the product. I mean, we would hang out everyday. We would meet at our offices in North Hollywood, do casting session, eat burgers, (Don's favorite food), hang out with young actresses, go see obscure Blue Grass and Alt Country bands at night, but rarely would we film. Maybe once a week we would actually break out the cameras and get something shot.

For example, it took us months-upon-months to film *Roller Blade Seven. Guns of Chupacabra* went on for over a year. I remember when we were filming the scenes at the *Cinco de Mayo* celebration at *Olvera Street,* I looked at Don and said, *"Remember we started filming this movie over a year ago in January."* He just shook his head.

That was the way it was working with him. The other problem was, once we did film something, he would hide the footage away until it was an absolute necessity to finish a film before he would turn it over to me to edit. As he held the purse strings, he was in control.

This is why, soon before he passed away, when he was in the hospitable, he made sure his wife turned over all of the footage to me, as there were so many films yet to be edited. I immediately started editing and did my duty to his legacy. That is why more films involving Donald G. Jackson came out after his death than while he was alive. And, for the record, there are a number of films created by either DGJ or myself or us as team that are out there that no one but the initiated have figured out that they are us using different names. Anyway…

The thing about being in association with Don was, there was always a price to pay. I said that while he was alive, (to his face), and after he died. Perhaps his mindset and the far-reaching implications of his behavior were all optimized during the period of time when we made *The Roller Blade Seven*. …Though I cover the process of making *The Roller Blade Seven,* the first Zen Film, pretty well in a chapter in my book, *Zen Filmmaking,* I think that it is almost necessary that I write another extended account, at some point, *Roller Blade Seven: The Darkness In The Light,* because a lot of bad things happened in association with that film, intermixed with good things all based on the behavior of Don. …Things that have traveled forward to today.

Perhaps an ideal illustration of what was to come was shown to me on the very first day, on the very first set, that involved Don and I. It was for the film, *Roller Blade 3*. Check out the doc I made about the film if you care to… Anyway, I had met Don shortly before that and he had asked me to star in the film. I arrived on the set, as did all of the rest of the cast and the crew. The female lead asked me if I wanted to run our lines, as it was a script-based production. I said, *"I'm a natural actor. I don't really do that. Let's just wait till we get on set and let it happen."* See… I was *Zen Filmmaking* before there was *Zen Filmmaking*.

In any case, on that day, I went looking for Don as nobody knew where he was. I found him outside, taking all of the junk he had in the trunk of his 1962 Plymouth and setting in on the ground of the parking lot. And, there was a lot of stuff in there! *"Just thought I would get this all in order,"* he stated. He was doing this while the cast and crew walked around with no direction. Organizing the junk in his trunk… That situation provided a very clear illustration of who that man was.

I always believe that life provides you with signs as what is to come if you are aware enough to watch for them. In the case of Donald G. Jackson, my first thought was to bail that fiasco, as up until that point in my career I had been working on high-budget or at least very organized independent productions. But, I stayed and it led to what it led to… *Zen Filmmaking*.

Am I sorry I stayed? No, not at all. But, as stated, there was always a price to pay and that price was often times quite high. But, from my staying, for better or for worse, *Zen Filmmaking* was born.

In closing, Don and I were very yin and yang—very different parts of the same puzzle. Me, I am about completion. I like to get it done. …Because then you have accomplished something. Don was not like that.

Life is always a battle between: process verse product. Modern Spirituality commonly provides people with the excuse, *"Enjoy the process."* Sure, enjoy it, but many people use that as a life-excuse for not making things happen and/or getting things done.

If you don't get it done, then it's not done. What have you accomplished?

So, if I must state one firm premise of *Zen Filmmaking,* that premise is, in *Zen Filmmaking* you get your project completed.

If you're not a filmmaker, this ideology doesn't only apply to filmmaking, it applies to everything.

Think about what you are doing. Think about why you are doing it. Contemplate what will it equal. Then, if you're going to do it, do it. Finish it. Make something special that is uniquely your own.

FADE OUT.

THE
ZEN

www.ingramcontent.com/pod-product-compliance
Lightning Source LLC
Chambersburg PA
CBHW020746160426

43192CB00006B/257